Table of Contents

Introduction

America is a country rich in diversity. A variety of landscapes are contained within its borders: mountains, deserts, plains, swamps, lakes, and even rain forests. The land and its resources have always dictated where people live and work. We've shaped the land, and in turn been shaped by it. Gathered within our borders is a multitude of cultures and voices. Everyone has his or her own individual story to tell. But as Americans, we have collective stories to tell—shared events which have changed the course of this country and, consequently, our own lives.

The goal of this book is to dramatize some of the events that have been turning points in our country's history. The ten plays presented here don't constitute a top-ten list of important events, but they do demonstrate how America is constantly evolving, always striving to live up to its promise of "life, liberty, and the pursuit of happiness." As the plays show, none of the events portrayed here occurred in a vacuum; the importance of cause and effect of the events is stressed. Each event had its own consequences—consequences which we feel today. Watershed events in our history have grown out of a desire to bring America to its full potential—both physically in the use of its resources (e.g., the Spanish explorations and the pioneers' westward expansion) and morally in the form of liberty and rights (e.g., the women's rights conventions and the civil-rights movement).

The scope of this collection has been dictated as well by the interests of the playwrights themselves. The nineteenth century, in particular, is well represented in this collection. It was a time when America grew physically in area and in the realization of what it meant to be a democracy. We endured both the Trail of Tears and the Oregon Trail. Women, denied the vote due to perceived weakness, were trekking across the country. Opposing voices play a strong role in these plays. For instance, not all American colonists wanted to boot out the British; not all women wanted the vote. Turning points are characterized by difficult decisions and concentrated action. One of the goals of these plays is to help students better understand the difficult decisions people have made in the past. Students may then begin to see themselves as participants in the history of their country and the world, and come to realize that history is an ongoing process—it's happening to them, now.

Description of Plays and Teaching Guide

This collection has been designed to enrich your existing curriculum. Since these plays can be read aloud as well as acted, incorporating them into your classroom will strengthen oral literacy and reading skills. Knowing that they can read the plays aloud may lessen some students' anxiety about performing. Those students who enjoy acting can personalize their roles with body movement.

Everyone should be encouraged to take on a role and participate in the cooperative effort of the group. Rotate roles so everyone has a chance to appear in a play. This can be a great way to spawn discussion. Girls may protest that they can't play male roles; boys

★ 10 ★
American History Plays
For the Classroom

Edited by Sarah J. Glasscock

SCHOLASTIC
PROFESSIONAL BOOKS

New York • Toronto • London • Auckland • Sydney

Acknowledgments

The editor wishes to thank the imaginative and dedicated playwrights whose work appears in this collection. Extra special thanks go to Mary Pat Champeau and Virginia Dooley for their support, expertise, and commitment.

Cover design by Vincet Ceci and Jaime Lucero
Interior design by Frank Maiocco
Photo Research by Daniella Jo Nilva

Cover photos
Spanish exploration, Thanksgiving, Boston Tea Party, Trail of Tears, and Pearl Harbor:
The Granger Collection; Ellis Island: Brown Brothers.

Interior photos
7, 16, 26, 35, 43, 52, 79: The Granger Collection; 62: Archive Photos; 69: Brown Brothers; 88: Associated Press.

ISBN 0-590-59931-3

may resist female roles. Although race and gender are often specific and important in the events described, they don't matter in the casting of the plays. In fact, playing characters very different from themselves may deepen students' insight into the times and events depicted.

A teaching guide follows each play. The guide begins with the **What Happened?** section which gives historical background on the event and provides further context. Two bibliographies are included: **Read All About It!** focuses on literature about the event itself, while **Read Some More!** includes literature about topics related to the event. In the **ACTIVITIES** section, there are ideas for cross-curricular activities that emphasize discussion, writing, research, and cooperative learning. Small groups or the entire class may participate in the discussion activities. Many writing activities center around individual writing, but students should be encouraged to share their work with their classmates. Also, small groups may want to collaborate on writing projects and create a book of their work. A small group may also tackle a research project; members may undertake different topics or avenues and then come together in the group to collate their information.

The teaching guide is exactly that—a guide. Feel free to use it as a starting point and expand any of the sections. Encourage students to create activities that correspond to their own interests. You may want to broaden the scope of this book by having students research and then write their own plays about other events in American history. The books below contain an overview of American history and can help launch the students' own works.

> *America in Time: America's History Year by Year Through Text and Pictures.*
>   Malcolm C. Jensen. Boston,: Houghton Mifflin, 1971.
> *America Alive: A History.* Jean Karl. New York: Philomel Books, 1994.
> *Read More About It, Volume 3: An Encyclopedia of Information Sources on
> Historical Figures and Events.* Ann Arbor, MI: the Pierian Press, 1989.

The series, *A History of Us* (Books 1-10) by Joy Hakim, which is published by Oxford University Press, is also an excellent source.

When to Put on the Plays

The plays in this book may be used in conjunction with your current social studies curriculum. A readers' theater format will also bolster your language arts program. The plays work well within the framework of thematic units. Another approach is to time productions based upon the anniversary of an event. Stage a reading of the play, and present the projects that arise out of the activities. (Although many plays span days and even years, a specific date can usually be fixed for an event.) The possibilities are as endless as your and your students' imaginations!

How to Put on the Plays

Before having students read through a play, make books suggested in the bibliography—and any others that you particularly like—available. Share the historical background of the event to provide students with a context. Because the plays are tailored for a wide audience, you and your students may find it helpful to cull a vocabulary list from the text. After a first read-through of the play, you may want to assign the activities, especially the ones involving discussion to get students talking about the event and the way in which it was portrayed. And, depending upon how elaborate your productions get, some of the writing and research activities can have an impact on the script, sets, and costumes. You may find that your students get more adventurous as they become comfortable with the structure of the plays and activities. Your class may go from simply reading the plays without any embellishments to putting on full-scale productions for schoolmates, families, and friends!

Again, the goal of these plays is to involve students—not only with the past but also with the present. Students should feel that they can be any of the characters—regardless of their own backgrounds or the character's. Some students may enjoy the role of the narrator. Others may blossom as they step into other people's lives. Some of the plays contain crowd scenes; these roles provide excellent opportunities for ad-libbing. The readers' theater format offers a non-threatening way to encourage student participation—and what better way to learn than by doing?

Spanish Exploration:
Cabeza de Vaca's Journey into the Unknown

By Jaime Lucero

Characters (in order of appearance):

NARRATORS 1–3

ÁLVAR NUÑEZ CABEZA DE VACA: Royal treasurer
of Narvaez expedition

ESTAVANICO: Moorish man enslaved by the Spaniards

GOVERNOR PAMFILO DE NARVAEZ: Leader of expedition

ALONSO DEL CASTILLO: Member of expedition

VASCO PORCALLO: Merchant in Trinidad

SEA PILOT

ALONSO ENRIQUEZ: Comptroller of expedition
(A comptroller is in charge of expenses.)

ANDRES DORANTES: Member of expedition

TIMUCUAN INDIANS 1-2 (nonspeaking roles)

CAPOQUE INDIANS 1-3 (nonspeaking roles)

ACT 1

Scene 1: About November, 1527, in Santiago de Cuba.

NARRATOR 1: Álvar Nuñez Cabeza de Vaca was born in about 1490 (two years before Christopher Columbus sailed to North America) in a small town in Spain. The name Cabeza de Vaca which means "head of cow" was given to one of his ancestors as a noble rank. During a war in Spain, this ancestor guided his army to safety by marking a secret mountain pass with a cow's head.

NARRATOR 2: In his teens, Cabeza de Vaca began a military career. At the age of 37, he was asked to join Pamfilo de Narvaez's expedition for the conquest of Florida. The expedition consisted of five ships and 300 men. Cabeza de Vaca was appointed royal treasurer and second in command. The expedition set sail on June 17, 1527.

NARRATOR 3: After three rough months at sea and before arriving in Florida, the expedition landed on the islands of Santo Domingo and Cuba to gather supplies, arms, and horses. The men—many sick and unhappy—were excited to finally see land. It's no wonder that many of the crew fled.

CABEZA DE VACA: Governor, we've lost almost half the men. We must leave immediately before we lose any more.

ESTAVANICO: Plus the natives are saying that the bad weather season's approaching.

NARVAEZ: Nonsense! We haven't completed our work here.

DORANTES: With all due respect, Governor, we've been here for 45 days. We've loaded as much as the ships can carry.

NARVAEZ: Wrong! There's more to come. A very important gentleman—Vasco Porcallo, maybe you've heard of him?—has agreed to help with more supplies. Except that we must pick them up in Trinidad. I want you, Cabeza de Vaca, and you, Castillo, to go. Take two ships and plenty of men.

CASTILLO: This little side trip's going to throw the whole expedition off schedule!

CABEZA DE VACA: Castillo's right. We have enough of everything. And Florida is so close!

NARVAEZ: I think you're forgetting who's in command here. (*snapping his fingers*) Now, go!

(Narvaez leaves.)

CASTILLO (*to Cabeza de Vaca*): You should be in command.

CABEZA DE VACA: Well, I'm not. And an order's an order. Tomorrow we set sail for Trinidad.

Scene 2: Several days later; in the Port of Trinidad.

NARRATOR 1: Cabeza de Vaca, Castillo, and a crew of men carried out Narvaez's order. When they arrived in Trinidad, Porcallo was there to greet them.

PORCALLO: Welcome!

CABEZA DE VACA (*shaking Porcallo's hand*): Nice to meet you. We'd like to load the supplies immediately and be on our way.

PORCALLO: No need to hurry!

SEA PILOT (*overhearing the conversation*): Get out of here as fast as you can! This is a bad port! A very bad port! It eats ships!

PORCALLO: Nonsense! If a ship goes down, it's obviously the pilot's fault.

SEA PILOT (*shaking his head*): The *Granada*, the *Ferdinand*, the *Santiago* . . . lost! All lost! Eaten up!

CASTILLO (*to Cabeza de Vaca*): I don't like the looks of that sky. I think we're headed for a storm.

CABEZA DE VACA: It doesn't look good. But when it hits, we may be safer here in port than out at sea.

PORCALLO: A few clouds—nothing more! Maybe we get a little rain—that's it!

SEA PILOT: Leave while you can! What good are supplies when you're at the bottom of the sea?

NARRATOR 2: The following morning a violent storm—the most severe storm that any of the men had ever experienced—struck the island. Of this hurricane, Cabeza de Vaca would later write, "Nothing so terrible as this had been seen in these parts before." Cabeza de Vaca lost the two ships, 60 men, 20 horses, and most of the supplies.

NARRATOR 3: Several days later, Narvaez and the rest of the expedition arrived in Trinidad to pick up Cabeza de Vaca and the few survivors. Unnerved by what had happened, everyone agreed to spend the winter in Cuba. The expedition didn't set sail for Florida until February 20 of the following year. During this time, more crew members deserted.

ACT 2

Scene: April 12, 1528; Florida (perhaps Sarasota Bay).

NARRATOR 1: On its way to Florida, the expedition again fell victim to several violent storms.

NARRATOR 2: Several weeks later, Cabeza de Vaca and the Narvaez expedition spotted land—and houses, thought to belong to Indians. Upon landing, Narvaez instructed Alonso Enriquez to pay these Indians a visit.

(Two Timucuan Indians holding spears squat behind bushes. Alonso Enriquez walks toward them, holding his hands up in the air—a sign that he carries no weapon. Standing a safe distance behind him, the other members of the expedition look on.)

ALONSO ENRIQUEZ (waving): Hello . . . hello. We come in peace.

(The Timucuan Indians look at each other.)

ENRIQUEZ (*signaling for them to come out from behind the bushes*): Come out!

NARVAEZ (*shouting to Enriquez*): Tell them we bring no harm! Show them your hands!

ENRIQUEZ (*muttering under his breath*): What do you think I'm doing? (then in a loud voice) We mean you no harm!

(The Indians again look at each other and then slowly walk out from behind the bushes. Enriquez smiles nervously when they finally reach him.)

NARVAEZ (*shouting*): Ask them where we can find food!

NARRATOR 3: Suddenly, the Timucuan began shouting at Enriquez and violently pointing at the sea, as if warning everyone to leave. Then they ran toward their village.

NARVAEZ (*hurrying up to Enriquez*): What happened? What did you do?

ENRIQUEZ: You saw. They don't want us here.

NARVAEZ: Nonsense! Where's the flag? (*A crew member puts a flagpole bearing the Spanish flag in his hands. Narvaez spikes the flag into the ground.*) In the name of King Charles V and the Queen of Spain, I claim this land.

CABEZA DE VACA: Sir, you're not thinking of exploring inland now?

NARVAEZ: And why shouldn't I?

ENRIQUEZ: We haven't secured the ships yet.

CABEZA DE VACA: Enriquez is right, I think we should continue sailing along the coast until we find a safe location—

NARVAEZ: The ships are fine here.

DORANTES: Sir, with all due respect, we don't know whether the natives will welcome us.

NARVAEZ: I think you're all forgetting who's in charge here. I say we unpack and make our camp here. Now, get to it!

EVERYONE: Yes, sir.

NARRATOR 1: As the crew unpacked, two arrows were shot at them. The arrows pierced a crate that Cabeza de Vaca was carrying. The two Timucuan Indians have returned with reinforcements.

CABEZA DE VACA (*taking cover behind the crate*): Everyone take cover! We're under attack!

(*All the men immediately scramble behind the crates. Narvaez dives behind the crate beside Cabeza de Vaca.*)

NARVAEZ: Round up the men! We're leaving!

NARRATOR 2: Unwelcome, the expedition quickly evacuated the land and then sailed west along the Gulf of Mexico. The Timucuan Indians followed on foot to make sure the ships didn't dock again.

NARRATOR 3: The ships sailed along the coast for months. But they were unable to find a safe place to land.

ACT 3

Scene 1: Winter, 1528. Off the coast of what is now Texas.

NARRATOR 1: Bad weather hit again. Cabeza de Vaca's ship was separated from the others. It capsized in the huge waves. By some miracle, Cabeza de Vaca and Dorantes were washed ashore on the same beach. Unconscious, they lay face down in the sand.

CABEZA DE VACA (*slowly waking up and spotting Dorantes*): Dorantes! Dorantes!

DORANTES (*groggy, finally opening his eyes*): Huh? Where are we? What happened?

11

CABEZA DE VACA (*hearing a noise*): Sshh!

DORANTES: What!

NARRATOR 2: Cabeza de Vaca, motioning for Dorantes to be quiet, crawled to the top of a sand dune and then peered cautiously over the top. To Dorantes' alarm, Cabeza de Vaca started to laugh. Castillo and Estavanico tumbled over the top of the sand dune and landed beside Dorantes. They clapped each other on the back.

DORANTES: You should let people know that you're hanging around.

CASTILLO (*turning serious*): We lost the others.

DORANTES AND CABEZA DE VACA: What?!

ESTAVANICO: The others went down with the ship. They drowned.

CASTILLO (to Cabeza de Vaca): I guess I got my wish, sir. You're in command now.

ESTAVANICO: We're the only ones left. The other ships won't ever find us.

DORANTES: Uh-oh . . .

NARRATOR 3: Several Capoque Indians had been tracking the survivors. They swooped over the sand dunes and surrounded Cabeza de Vaca and his men. Jabbing the air with their spears, the Capoque convinced the shipwrecked men to accompany them to their camp.

Scene 2: Later that morning. At the Capoque campsite.

NARRATOR 1: The four Spaniards are escorted into the Capoque camp. A wounded Capoque lay on the ground. Obviously in pain, he groaned. Cabeza de Vaca's captors pointed to the man. Then they touched the points of their spears to Cabeza de Vaca's chest.

CABEZA DE VACA (*to his men*): They want us to make him well.

CASTILLO: What?!

DORANTES: You mean, they think we're doctors?

CABEZA DE VACA: I believe so.

NARRATOR 2: Estavanico and Cabeza de Vaca knelt before the sick man. Cabeza de Vaca held his hand against the sick man's forehead to check for a fever. Estavanico looked at the wound. Castillo and Dorantes, terrified, stood still.

CASTILLO: Don't hurt him!

CABEZA DE VACA: He has a very high fever. How does the wound look, Estavanico?

ESTAVANICO: It's not bleeding. But maybe we should clean it.

CABEZA DE VACA: Good idea. Get them to heat some water. Castillo, Dorantes, come over here.

CASTILLO: But sir, I'm no doctor.

DORANTES: Me neither.

CABEZA DE VACA: If you want to stay alive, I suggest you start acting like one.

CASTILLO AND DORANTES (*gulping*): Yes sir!

CABEZA DE VACA: You can pray, can't you?

CASTILLO AND DORANTES: Yes sir!

CABEZA DE VACA: Then start praying.

NARRATOR 3: Amazingly, the Capoque man recovered. News of the "miraculous healers" spread. Soon, other villagers came to the Spaniards for treatment for their illnesses.

NARRATOR 1: Cabeza de Vaca later wrote in his journal: "Our method was to bless the sick, breathe upon them, recite a Pater Noster and Ave Maria, and pray earnestly to God our Lord for their recovery." In exchange for curing their people, the Capoque gave the Spaniards skins and food. There was, however, one drawback—Cabeza de Vaca and his men weren't allowed to leave. And as time progressed, it became clear that they were slaves to the Capoque people.

NARRATOR 2: Cabeza de Vaca later fled from the Capoque. It's believed that he went as far north as what is now Oklahoma. He lived with the Charruco people for several years, then moved on to live with many other native groups. News of his "healing powers" gained him acceptance with the people. Estavanico, Castillo, and Dorantes stayed with the Capoque. The four Spaniards met again six years later.

NARRATOR 3: In the ten years he spent in North America, Cabeza de Vaca journeyed across what are now Florida, Texas, New Mexico, Arizona, and northern Mexico. He returned to Spain on August 9, 1537. He published his journal in 1542 under the title: La Relación. Cabeza de Vaca's account of his travels is a rich source of firsthand information on the pre-European Southwest—the climate, plant and animal life, and the customs of the peoples living there.

What Happened?

 Álvar Nuñez Cabeza de Vaca was born in Jerez de la Frontera (a small Spanish town) in about 1490. His unique surname, which means "head of cow," originated as a title of honor given to an ancestor who used a cow's skull to mark an unguarded pass—which ultimately led the armies to safety. In 1527, Cabeza de Vaca joined Pamfilo de Narvaez and 300 men on a journey to North America. Their mission: to conquer Florida under the name of the king and queen of Spain. Unfortunately, due to Narvaez's careless leadership, unfriendly natives, and bad weather, the mission fell apart. Ultimately, Cabeza de Vaca lost contact with the exploration party and was shipwrecked with three other men on what is now the Texas coast. Enslaved by the Capoque people, Cabeza de Vaca eventually made his escape. He traveled on foot across Texas, New Mexico, Arizona, and northern Mexico.

The survivors were re-united again and managed to make it to New Galicia, a Spanish province in Mexico. There, the men related the tales they heard of the seven cities of Cíbola, where gold and silver was plentiful. Cabeza de Vaca returned to Spain, but Estavanico remained in Mexico. Two years later, in 1538, Francisco Vásquez Coronado became the governor of this province. Guided by Estavanico, Fray Marco de Niza, a priest, left New Galicia in search of the legendary cities. On their return to the province, they insisted that they had found evidence to support the legend. The two made one more attempt to find Cíbola. Estavanico was killed, but Fray Marco de Niza survived. Convinced of the existence of the cities of gold, Coronado received permission to mount an expedition to find the cities. He beat out both Hernando Cortés and Hernando de Soto. Part of the expedition reached the Grand Canyon, and the Spaniards came across the first herds of buffalo they'd ever seen; but the cities of Cíbola were never discovered.

Cabeza de Vaca's journal documenting the 10-year odyssey was published in 1542 under the title La Relación. Cabeza de Vaca died in 1557.

📖 Read All About It!

Brendt, Keith. *Cabeza de Vaca: New World Explorer*. Mahwah, NJ: Troll, 1993.
The Account: Alvar Núñez Cabeza de Vaca's Relación. José B. Fernández and Martín A.
    Favata, ed. and trans. Houston: Arte Público, 1993.
Wade, Mary D. *Cabeza de Vaca: Conquistador Who Cared*. Houston: Colophon House, 1994.

📖 Read Some More!

Arrington, Carol. *Estevanico: Black Explorer in Spanish Texas*. Austin: Eakin Press, 1986.
Merino, Jose Maria. *The Gold of Dreams*. New York: Farrar, Straus & Giroux, 1991.

ACTIVITIES

Home Sweet Home

What kept Cabeza de Vaca going all those years when he was lost in the desert? What sort of characteristics would a person need in order to survive in a land so foreign to him or her? Display a globe of the earth. Ask students to locate the places they feel are the most remote, and discuss their choices. Then talk about the geography of the place and how it would affect someone's ability to survive.

If It Weren't for—

Weather played an important role in the fate of the Narvaez expedition. Poor Judgment, too, affected the outcome. Which of the two do students feel had more of an impact: natural or human forces? Do they think that the shipwreck off the coast of Texas could have been avoided? What would have had to happen differently?

Gold!

Some of the Spanish explorers in the Southwest were searching for gold. Estavanico lost his life pursuing the fabled seven cities of Cíbola. Legends abound about lost gold mines hidden in remote mountain peaks. Guide students in locating examples of these legends. Then have them rewrite the tales in their own words and include a moral at the end. Note: *Coronado's Children: Tales of Lost Mines and Buried Treasures of the Southwest* by J. Frank Dobie (Austin: University of Texas Press, 1981) is a good resource for these legends, but preview it before making it available to your class.

Journal Jottings

Cabeza de Vaca wrote a journal about his travels across the Southwest. Invite students to take a walk in an unfamiliar area in their neighborhood, keeping a journal as they go along. What do they see, hear, or smell? What strikes them about the people, the buildings, the weather? Ask students to pretend they're seeing these things for the first time. You may want to share portions of Cabeza de Vaca's La Relación with students.

Charting Cabeza de Vaca's Course

Although Cabeza de Vaca recorded the sights and sounds of his journey, historians disagree over the exact route he took through the Southwest. (The Arte Público translation of the journal is a good source for the different routes.) Ask students to find at least one map showing Cabeza de Vaca's route. After they retrace the route on a current U.S. road map, have them calculate the number of miles that Cabeza de Vaca covered on foot. How long would that same journey take by car today?

Stormy Weather

Cabeza de Vaca and Castillo were lucky that they reached the port of Trinidad before the hurricane blew in. Put students in charge of an expedition sailing from Cuba, Trinidad, or Santo Domingo to Florida. They must consider the best season in which to travel. To do this, ask them to research hurricanes. By studying the most severe storms, and the times of year and the places they hit, can they find a pattern? What kind of emergency equipment will the boat need in the event of an unexpected storm?

The Pilgrims' Arrival:
Thanksgiving at Plymouth

By Sarah Glasscock

Characters (in order of appearance):

NARRATOR

MARY ALLERTON: a Separatist

ISAAC ALLERTON: a Separatist

REMEMBER ALLERTON: a Separatist boy

LITTLE MARY ALLERTON: a Separatist girl

MILES STANDISH: a Stranger

MAYFLOWER CREW MEMBERS 1-2

SEPARATISTS 1-3 (nonspeaking roles)

STRANGERS 1-3 (nonspeaking roles)

SAMOSET: an Abenaki

MASSASOIT: Chief of the Wampanoag people

SQUANTO: a Patuxet

WAMPANOAGS 1-3 (nonspeaking roles)

JOHN CARVER: First governor of Plymouth

WILLIAM BRADFORD: Second governor of Plymouth

ROSE STANDISH: a Stranger married to Miles Standish

Scene 1: November 11, 1620. On the deck of the Mayflower, which is anchored off the coast of Cape Cod.

NARRATOR: For the first time in 66 days, the passengers of the *Mayflower* are allowed up on deck. About half of the people on board are Separatists, or Pilgrims, who have come to this new land in search of religious freedom. The other half (about 50 people) are Strangers (the name given to them by the Pilgrims), servants, and hired men. The Strangers have left England to pursue a better economic life. Everyone's excited to see land, but trouble's brewing . . .

MARY: Cape Cod! But that means we're off the coast of New England!

ISAAC: Ah, just look at it, Mary. It's land all the same.

REMEMBER: I see a tiger! Look—on the beach!

LITTLE MARY: Where? I don't see anything.

REMEMBER: It's gone now.

NARRATOR: Miles Standish, one of the Strangers, overhears the Allertons' conversation as he strolls by. He gives Isaac Allerton a hearty pat on the back.

MILES: Mary's right. We're supposed to land in Virginia, not New England. Our contract says Virginia. If this isn't Virginia, then the contract's no good. We can do anything we want—

MARY: A little prayer wouldn't hurt you, Miles Standish.

MILES: You'd have us on our knees, praying from noon till midnight if you could.

ISAAC: Now, now.

NARRATOR: Two crew members come up to the railing and crowd the Allertons and Standish. They fiddle with the ropes and pretend to be adjusting knots.

MAYFLOWER CREW MEMBER 1 (*giving the Allertons and Standish a dark look*): Throw 'em all off, I say. It's land, ain't it?

MAYFLOWER CREW MEMBER 2: Aye. We've barely got enough food and supplies to get us and ourselves back to England.

MAYFLOWER CREW MEMBER 1: If they want Virginia, then they'll have to find her using their own two legs and carrying their own food.

(Mary pulls the children close to her. Isaac and Miles exchange looks. Satisfied, the two sailors head for another group of Pilgrims and Strangers.)

MILES (*in a booming voice*): New England! Full of trees! Do you know how many barrels John Alden can make out of all those trees? Look at that ocean! Full of fish! Do you know how many of those fish those barrels will hold? Why, there'll be no stopping us.

REMEMBER: Would his barrels hold a tiger?

MILES: Absolutely! And just to prove it—I'm going to catch that tiger and ship it across the sea to King James.

MARY: And who would get the blame when it ate up the king? Not you, or any of the other Strangers. We would. You can joke about it all you want, Miles Standish. You haven't been thrown into jail for your beliefs. You haven't been hanged.

MILES: Now, Mary, if I'd been hanged, how could I be here at all?

(Isaac bends down to whisper into his son Remember's ear. Then the boy runs off to another group of passengers.)

ISAAC: Enough, you two. We have serious things to discuss.

Scene 2. That evening. The Great Cabin of the Mayflower. Pilgrims and Strangers—men, women, and children—are crowded into the cabin.

NARRATOR: Messengers have run back and forth between the Pilgrims and Strangers all morning and afternoon. At last it's agreed that some sort of document should be drawn up to spell out how they should rule themselves. The Pilgrims want to guarantee their religious freedom. The Strangers want the freedom to follow their own religious beliefs, and not the Pilgrims'.

A set of rules and laws are finally agreed to and written down. Isaac Allerton is the last Separatist man to sign this document, known as the Mayflower Compact. He holds out the pen to Miles Standish.

ISAAC: Miles? I'd be honored to have your name signed with mine.

(Standish takes his time. He looks at every Stranger in the room as if he is taking a silent vote.)

MILES: England's an ocean away. I guess we're stuck with each other.

NARRATOR: Miles Standish signs the compact. One by one, the remaining men—the rest of the Strangers from the richest to the poorest, their male servants, and the hired men—add their names to the paper. At this time, English women had no separate, legal voice. None of the women's names appear on the Mayflower Compact.

In the first order of business, the men elect John Carver to be the colony's governor.

ACT 2

Scene 1: March 16, 1621. The woods surrounding the town of Plymouth. Mary and Remember Allerton are playing and collecting sticks of firewood. They don't see Samoset, who is watching them from behind a tree and enjoying their games.

NARRATOR: Exploring parties go out to search for a good site to build a town. Some find seed corn buried in baskets and take the corn back to the Mayflower. In late December of 1620, a party finds site with a stream near it and abandoned fields of corn—the site was once a Patuxet Indian village. The Pilgrims and Strangers agree to build their town here, at Plymouth.

That first winter is hard. Many people die of illness—probably either tuberculosis or pneumonia, but the building goes on. A Common House is raised first. After that, about five or six rough houses are finished.

Then, in the spring, a visitor arrives.

REMEMBER: Okay, count how many sticks you have. Whoever has the most sticks gets to have honey with their bread tonight. I have 223 sticks.

LITTLE MARY: How many do I have to have to beat you?

REMEMBER: I have 223 sticks, so you need 1,011 sticks.

LITTLE MARY: How many sticks do I have?

REMEMBER: One, two, three, four, five . . . ummm, you have maybe ten sticks. So, you need about . . . a thousand more sticks.

LITTLE MARY: Oh!

SAMOSET (*stepping into the open and placing a stick on Mary's pile*): Now, only 999 more sticks. (*Remember freezes.*) Try counting your pile again, little brother. Looks more like 12 sticks to me.

REMEMBER: You're—you—you're, you're an Indian!

LITTLE MARY: Oh! Do I have to give the stick back to him?

REMEMBER: Hey—wait a minute! Wait just a minute. I can understand him. He's not an Indian. He's speaking English.

SAMOSET: We can talk in my language if you want to—you speak any Abenaki?

REMEMBER: No . . . but I know some Dutch.

SAMOSET: You got me there. I bet my friend Squanto does, though. He's been to England—and Spain. Might be he picked up some Dutch along the way.

LITTLE MARY: Is Squanto an Indian?

SAMOSET: He's a Patuxet. They used to live here, where your village is. Those were their corn fields.

REMEMBER: Uh-oh. Are they going to want everything back?

SAMOSET: They're all dead. Some sickness. Squanto's the only Patuxet left. Maybe it's a good thing he got kidnapped and taken across the ocean. So who's in charge around here?

REMEMBER: Ummm, we've got a governor . . .

SAMOSET: Sounds good. Take me to your governor.

NARRATOR: Remember and Mary Allerton lead Samoset to the Common House in Plymouth. A business meeting is being held inside. Alarmed guards bar the door. "Welcome, Englishmen," Samoset says, and then he introduces himself. The surprised Englishmen agree to a meeting with Massasoit, the most powerful leader in the area and chief of the Wampanoag people. Samoset also promises to bring Squanto.

Scene 2: March 22, 1621. Outside the Plymouth meeting house. The people of Plymouth are awaiting the arrival of Massasoit.

MILES: I'm not saying I don't trust Samoset or this Massasoit. I'm a soldier. A soldier's job is to be prepared.

GOVERNOR CARVER: Just make sure none of your men start waving their swords around.

MILES: I just want the Indians to know that they'll pay if they keep stealing our tools.

REMEMBER (*running up to his father*): They're coming! They're coming! Hundreds of them!

ISAAC: Did you see Samoset?

REMEMBER (*nodding*): Yes, he's near the front of the group.

NARRATOR: Massasoit and his group move slowly into the Common. Governor Carver gives a signal. The sounds of drums and a trumpet fill the air. Carver recognizes Massasoit's power and authority by kissing the Wampanoag leader's hand. Samoset walks from group to group, greeting the colonists. He turns to introduce Squanto, but Squanto is looking around his old home.

GOVERNOR CARVER: Your visit is a great honor, Massasoit. We have many things to talk about.

MILES: Missing tools, for one! (*sticking out his hand for Massasoit to shake*) Miles Standish, Chief.

MASSASOIT (*ignoring Standish's hand*): Nice red hair. You must be the one who stole the corn from the Pamets. Dug it right up and took their baskets, too.

GOVERNOR CARVER (*hastily*): You must be hungry and thirsty after your trip, Massasoit. Let's have some refreshment before we talk.

NARRATOR: The English and the Wampanoag are curious about each other. But they are suspicious of each other, too. After everyone has had something to eat and to drink, the two groups sit down together. Massasoit and Governor Carver, with the help of Squanto who interprets for them, discuss many things.

MASSASOIT: We believe in peace. We welcome you. But we've welcomed others like you before. You kidnap us. You bring sickness to us. Look at what you've done to Squanto. Look at what you've done to his village.

GOVERNOR CARVER: We come in peace, to live here in peace. We know what it's like to be hunted and to lose our homes.

SQUANTO (*to Massasoit*): What he says is true.

MASSASOIT: Then we must help each other. You pay for the corn you took—you'll get your tools back. If any of my people hurt you, I will punish them. I ask you to do the same.

GOVERNOR CARVER: Agreed. We will not take from each other or fight each other.

MASSASOIT: And if someone attacks you, I will take your side. If someone attacks me, will you take mine?

MILES: No sir! We're not responsible for what got stirred up before we got here!

GOVERNOR CARVER: We are friends. An attack on you is an attack on me.

NARRATOR: The peace treaty between the Plymouth community and the Wampanoags lasts for the next 50 years. Massasoit and his group leave the next day, but Squanto stays behind.

ACT 3

Scene 1: Late spring, 1621. The fields around Plymouth.

NARRATOR: Squanto teaches the Plymouth settlers many things: how to catch fish in the brook, how to use the fish as fertilizer in the fields, the best way to plant corn, and how to tap the sap in the maple trees. He also guides them on expeditions around the countryside and along the coast. And sometimes, Squanto talks about his own life.

SQUANTO (*dropping kernels of seed corn into the ground*): One, two, three, four. Cover the corn.

REMEMBER: One, two, three, four. Cover the corn.

LITTLE MARY: One, two, three, four. Cover the corn.

SQUANTO: Good. Now we'll dig a hole for the herring.

LITTLE MARY (*eyeing Squanto doubtfully*): Will our corn taste like fish?

SQUANTO: No. It makes the corn taste more like corn. You'll see.

REMEMBER: Are you mad that we're here? That we're living where you used to live?

SQUANTO: My people are gone. If you had pushed them out of their village, then I'd be mad.

REMEMBER: But an English sea captain kidnapped you—does that mean you hate the English?

LITTLE MARY: If you hated us, then you might try to talk us into planting fish close to our corn.

SQUANTO: I don't hate anyone. I don't hate the English captain. I don't hate the Spanish priests he sold me to. I ran away from them, to England, but I don't hate them.

REMEMBER: Do you miss England a little bit? I do.

SQUANTO: A little bit.

LITTLE MARY: Are you going to run away from us, Squanto?

SQUANTO: This is my home. I won't leave it. No matter what anybody does to me.

REMEMBER: Maybe in about 50 years, we could go back and visit England. It might be safe for all of us by then.

SQUANTO: Maybe. Here—throw in your corn. Less talking and more planting.

Scene 2: Fall, 1621. Thanksgiving celebration in Plymouth.

NARRATOR: Thanks to Squanto, the harvest that fall was plentiful. The people of Plymouth decide to celebrate. They invite Massasoit, Samoset, and—of course—Squanto to their day of thanksgiving. Everyone attends, including 90 Wampanoag! The lawn in front of the Common House is filled with tables, and the tables are loaded with food: venison, duck, geese, turkeys, lobster, eel pie, corn bread, salad greens, and plums and berries.

MARY: Oh, no! There must be a hundred people with Massasoit! We don't have enough food for everyone!

ROSE: We'll just have to send the men out for more fish and game. I'll round up the children to get more berries and plums—

(Rose stops talking and smiles as Massasoit walks up to her and Mary Allerton.)

MASSASOIT: So much food! We've brought five deer for the feast, too. I hope that's not too much?

MARY (*relieved*): Oh, you shouldn't have!

NARRATOR: Everyone piles their plates high with food. But before eating, William Bradford the new governor of Plymouth offers his thanks to the guests.

GOVERNOR BRADFORD: We have suffered much this year, yet we have much to give thanks for. We have lost many friends, yet we have gained the friendship of Massasoit and his people, and of Samoset. We are most grateful that Squanto has returned to his home. He is truly God's blessing to us. Massasoit, would you say a few words?

MASSASOIT (*rising*): Every year, we give thanks, too, for our harvest. We call our celebration the Green Corn Dance. We may dress differently, we may call our celebrations by different names, but—sometimes, sometimes—we are not so different. Let's eat!

What Happened?

 During the reigns of Queen Elizabeth I and King James I, the only church in England was the Church of England. The queen or king was the head of the church. Speaking out against the church was considered the same as speaking out against the government. People could be jailed or even put to death. A group of people called the Separatists withdrew from the Church of England. Secretly, they formed their own church. In 1608, the Separatists fled to Holland, where they could worship as they chose. But life was hard in Holland. The Separatists had been farmers in England. They had to learn new trades, such as carpentering and tailoring. Their children had to work, too.

And, as the years passed, the Separatists' church didn't grow as they had hoped. Many of the children were influenced by the freer Dutch life. The Separatists decided to move to the Virginia colony in North America. An English businessman offered to provide a ship and supplies if the Separatists would agree to send back merchandise from Virginia. The businessman also insisted that 40 English volunteers go to North America on the ship. These volunteers, called Strangers by the Separatists, included John Alden and Miles and Rose Standish.

On September 16, 1620, after several delays, the *Mayflower* sailed out of Plymouth, England. Sixty-six days later, land was spotted. Although they had landed off the shore of Cape Cod rather than Virginia, the settlers chose to remain in New England. They anchored in Provincetown Harbor but found that the land there could not support them. Before going ashore, the Pilgrims and Strangers forged a set of rules that would govern them. This document, known as the Mayflower Compact, set down the principles of self-rule. In December, they settled in what is now Plymouth, Massachusetts.

📖 Read All About It!

Bradford, William, and Others of the Mayflower Company. *Homes in the Wilderness: A Pilgrim's Journal of Plymouth Plantation in 1620*. North Haven, CT: Linnet, 1988.
Jassem, Kate. *Squanto, The Pilgrim Adventure*. Mahwah, NJ: Troll Associates, 1979.
San Souci, Robert. *N.C. Wyeth's Pilgrims*. San Francisco: Chronicle Books, 1991.
Siegel, Beatrice. *A New Look at Pilgrims: Why They Came to America*. New York: Walker and Company, 1987.

📖 Read Some More!

Bowen, Gary. *Stranded at Plimouth Plantation*. New York: HarperCollins Publishers, 1994.
Dorris, Michael. *Guests*. New York: Hyperion, 1994.
Peters, Russell M. *Clambake: A Wampanoag Tradition*. Minneapolis, MN: Lerner Publishing Company, 1992.

ACTIVITIES

Food for Thought

What was served at the first Thanksgiving? Roasted duck, turkeys, and deer; lobster pie, clams, oysters, and fish; nuts; dried wild plums, gooseberries, strawberries, cherries; hotcakes and biscuits; Indian pudding and popcorn balls. Which foods do your students associate with Thanksgiving? Involve students in planning a representative menu for a classroom Thanksgiving celebration. After completing your menu, discuss the things for which they are thankful this year.

Classroom Compact

The Mayflower Compact set down the rules by which the Pilgrims and Strangers agreed to live together. Because the two groups had different viewpoints on several issues, such as religion, this document helped avoid many problems and offered solutions for those problems that did arise. Suggest to your students that they create their own Classroom Compact to govern their own behavior. What kinds of rules are important in a classroom? How do individual rights affect those of the class as a whole, and vice versa? After a wide-ranging discussion, set down the rules in writing and have the class sign their compact. Then post the Classroom Compact.

Only the Necessities

Families packed their things in small chests to bring over on the *Mayflower*. The chests held blankets, clothes, and personal things. The families also brought cooking and sewing items. Bring a standard size moving carton to class. Ask students: If you were starting a new life in a strange place, what would you take with you? Then explain that their items must fit inside the moving carton. After students measure the carton, have them determine if their items will fit inside. Have them record their lists of items, measurements, determinations of fit, and packing plans in a journal.

The First Thing You Need to Know

Squanto taught the Plymouth colonists many things. His knowledge of his home's land, water, and climate helped save many newcomers' lives. Suppose someone who has never been to America moves into your community. What are the most important things for that person to know: How much the bus costs? How to dial 911? Where to buy the latest fashions? Let your class compile a how-to book for your community. They should provide detailed instructions and diagrams so that anyone will be able to use their book.

A Harvest of Celebrations

The Wampanoags had lived in America for hundreds of years before the *Mayflower* arrived. They celebrated harvest with the Green Corn Dance. Many groups of Native Americans lived throughout North America in 1620 (provide of map showing where the inhabitants of what is now America lived in the 1600s). Have individuals or groups focus on specific peoples. Students should find out what their daily lives were like and also how they celebrated. How did their harvests differ from the Pilgrims?

Who Was there?

Miles and Rose Standish were there. Squanto was there. So were the Allertons. Who else was at that first Thanksgiving in Plymouth? After deciding on one person to profile, students should prepare a biography. Then ask them to imagine to be that person, and create a first-person account of that Thanksgiving in 1621. They can open or close their biography with their accounts.

The Boston Tea Party:
The Night Boston Harbor Turned into a Giant Teapot

By Sarah Glasscock

CASTING TEA OVERBOARD IN BOSTON HARBOR.

Characters (in order of appearance):

WOMEN 1-2

MEN 1-3

SAM ADAMS: a Patriot

JOHN HANCOCK: a Patriot and merchant

BOYS AND MEN 1-5 (nonspeaking roles)

CAPTAIN OF THE DARTMOUTH

BRITISH OFFICER

BRITISH SOLDIERS 4-5 (nonspeaking roles)

HONOR TURNER: a Boston woman

ELIZABETH HARRISON: a Boston woman

GIRLS AND WOMEN 1-5 (nonspeaking roles)

THOMAS BOYLSTON: a Boston merchant

ACT 1

Scene 1: The night of December 16, 1773. Old South Church in Boston.

NARRATOR: Old South Church is filled with people. It's also filled with tension and excitement. Everyone is talking. Three ships—the *Dartmouth*, *Eleanor*, and *Beaver*—are anchored in Boston Harbor. The ships are filled with 90,000 pounds of tea, but the people of Boston won't take the tea. And the British won't let the ships leave and go to another port. Why? Listen—

WOMAN 1: I don't mind paying a bit of tax on my tea. It's the rest of it that I don't like.

WOMAN 2: I don't mind it at all. Only one company can bring in the tea, and they get to choose who sells it to us. So what? It's still tea, isn't it?

MAN 1: First it's tea—then what? They'll be putting a tax on going to church or talking to your friends on the street.

MAN 2: The British won't let Francis Rotch take the *Dartmouth* out of the harbor and sail her to another port. Francis doesn't want any trouble. He's willing to take his cargo somewhere else.

MAN 3: The British don't want any trouble. They'll let him leave. You'll see.

MAN 1: If they don't, we have a little surprise for them.

MAN 3 (*looking suspiciously at Man 1*): What do you mean?

WOMAN 1: Sshh! (*nudging Man 1*) There's Mr. Rotch now!

WOMAN 2: Look at him! Going right up to Sam Adams. Well, we're in trouble now. Sam Adams would pick a fight with a newborn kitten.

WOMAN 1: Oh, hush!

NARRATOR: The crowd inside the church is silent. Will the British let the three ships, still loaded with tea, sail out of Boston Harbor? They watch as Francis Rotch tells Sam Adams and John Hancock about his meeting with the British. Francis Rotch shakes his head each time Sam Adams asks him a question. Adams' face turns as red as his hair. A low murmur starts in the audience and grows.

SAM ADAMS (*standing up*): People of Boston! Friends! The British will not let Mr. Rotch take the *Dartmouth*—his own ship—out of Boston Harbor. They insist that we must take the tea. I'm sorry—they insist that we must buy the tea from their agents, and their agents only. They insist we must pay a tax on this tea. They insist that we are not free to

27

decide these things. (*pausing and then shaking his head*) Ladies and gentlemen—this meeting can do nothing more to save the country.

MAN 1 (*springing up*): They want us to take the tea? Then let's take it! We'll turn Boston Harbor into a teapot!

WOMAN 1: Aye, we'll hold a tea party the British won't ever forget!

MAN 2: To the Dartmouth! We'll free your ship, Mr. Rotch!

JOHN HANCOCK: Let every man do what is right in his own eyes!

NARRATOR: Shouting and talking excitedly, the people pour out of the church and head for Griffin's Wharf where the three ships are anchored.

Scene 2: Later that night at Griffin's Wharf in Boston Harbor where the Dartmouth, Eleanor, and Beaver are anchored.

NARRATOR: Three groups of men and boys carrying torches board the ships. Some have stopped long enough to darken their faces with ash and paint so they look like Indians. No one says a word. The people on the wharf are quiet, too, as they watch. They know that there's no turning back.

JOHN HANCOCK (*approaching the captain of the Dartmouth*): We won't harm you or your ship, sir. All we ask is that you stand aside.

CAPTAIN: I don't have a choice, do I?

JOHN HANCOCK: No. And neither do we. The British have decided for us.

NARRATOR: The Boston men go to work quickly. They bring up the chests of tea and dump their contents into the harbor. When all the chests are empty, the men sweep the decks of the ships. The people of Boston want to send a message to the British: They demand freedom and liberty, and will fight for it. But they believe in law and order, too.

ACT 2

Scene 1: May 10, 1774. Griffin's Wharf.

NARRATOR: The tea party in Boston angers King George III and the British. A new set of acts, or rules, is forced upon the people of Boston. At Griffin's Wharf, a crowd gathers to read the list of rules.

MAN 1: They can't do this!

WOMAN 1: We knew there'd be a price to pay for dumping the tea.

MAN 1: But this! This is intolerable! Closing the port of Boston until we pay for the tea! Moving the capital from here to Salem! Forbidding town meetings! Making us feed British soldiers and put them up in our homes!

WOMAN 1: They mean to starve us. They mean to close down our shops. If they close the harbor, no boats can come in or go out.

MAN 2: You've left out the worst one. They've taken away the colonial assembly from us. From now on, the governor chooses the members of the assembly. And who chooses the royal governor? Not us! We've lost our right to vote on the members. We've lost our voice.

WOMAN 2: A fine fix you've got us into. Dressing up like Indians and ruining perfectly good tea. Why pick a fight with England? We'll lose, and then what?

WOMAN 1: Can't you read, woman? They're taking away our rights. They're treating us like children. They want us to be good and keep quiet.

MAN 1: Aye, as long as we send them boats loaded with timber and fish and fur! They need us, our resources, more than we need them!

MAN 3 (*pointing to Woman 2*): No, she's right. We've got friends in England. The colonies will get representatives in Parliament if we go slowly. That'll be an end to that. No more taxation without representation. The colonies will have a voice in England. We'll have a say in how we're governed—

WOMAN 1: It's too late for that. He's right (nodding to Man 1 and then tapping the list of rules); these are intolerable. They're intolerable acts.

WOMAN 2: Don't say I didn't warn you. When you're on your knees, begging the British to forgive you, and they're not interested. Just don't say I didn't warn you.

MAN 1: If you love the British so much, why don't you—(*stops talking when Woman 1 elbows him*)

(*A group of British soldiers marches toward the crowd.*)

BRITISH OFFICER: Move on! Come on, move on, move on! You've had time enough to read. If it was up to me, I'd have you fish every single tea leaf out of the harbor. Move on, I said! Come on!

MAN 2 (*muttering*): If it was up to me, I'd stuff every single leaf of tea down your throat—all ninety thousand pounds of it.

BRITISH OFFICER: What's that!?

WOMAN 2: Nothing! He was just telling me to keep quiet and mind my own business.

(The crowd moves off together.)

Scene 2: Later in 1774. The warehouses along Griffin's Wharf.

NARRATOR: The British close Boston Harbor. Large amounts of coffee and sugar sit in some Boston warehouses. These goods arrived before the harbor was shut down. The owners of these warehouses are now charging high prices for the products. They think the people of Boston will have no choice but to pay the prices. The women of Boston disagree. One morning, they take matters into their own hands. A group of at least a hundred women march down to Thomas Boylston's warehouse. They're wheeling a large cart and smaller hand trucks.

JOHN HANCOCK (*hearing the noise and coming out of his office nearby*): Ladies! What's happening? Where are you going?

HONOR TURNER (*answering without stopping*): To Boylston's, for some coffee.

JOHN HANCOCK (*falling in step with Honor*): But he's charging an arm and leg—

HONOR TURNER: Oh, I think he'll come down on his price for us.

(The women stop in front of Boylston's warehouse.)

ELIZABETH HARRISON: Mr. Boylston! Mr. Thomas Boylston!

HONOR TURNER: We've come for your coffee!

THOMAS BOYLSTON (*coming out of the warehouse and then locking the door behind him*): Ladies! Good morning, good morning! One at a time, one at a time! Plenty of coffee! Price has gone up a bit, you know. Six shillings a pound.

ELIZABETH HARRISON: Your keys, please, Mr. Boylston. We've come for your coffee.

THOMAS BOYLSTON (*thinking she's joking and laughing*): Now, now, ladies. I'm a merchant. I must make my living. How will I feed my family if I give away my coffee?

HONOR TURNER: Six shilling for a pound of coffee! Shame on you! You're taking the food out of our children's mouths.

THOMAS BOYLSTON (*starting to realize the women are serious*): I didn't throw any tea overboard, ladies. If your children are hungry, it's your husbands' fault, not mine. (*He turns to re-enter his warehouse, but the women block his way.*)

ELIZABETH HARRISON: You're a greedy man, Mr. Boylston. It's money you love, not freedom or liberty or your family.

THOMAS BOYLSTON (*coldly*): You are free not to buy my coffee.

HONOR TURNER: We have not come here to buy your coffee, sir. We have come here to take it. Now, hand over the keys to the warehouse, and we'll be quick about it.

THOMAS BOYLSTON: I will not!

(*Elizabeth Harrison grabs Boylston by the neck and tosses him into the cart. Boylston looks around in a panic.*)

THOMAS BOYLSTON (*seeing John Hancock in the crowd*): Hancock! John Hancock! Help me!

JOHN HANCOCK: Oh, I would give up the keys if I were you, sir.

(*A group of women surround Boylston in the cart.*)

HONOR TURNER: We would like you to hand over the keys, Mr. Boylston. But if you will not, then we will take them from you.

THOMAS BOYLSTON: All right! All right! (*tossing the keys to the ground*) There! Go ahead and steal my coffee! You're no better than King George!

NARRATOR: Honor unlocks the warehouse. The women dump Boylston out of the cart. Then they wheel the empty cart into the warehouse. Inside the warehouse, they work as quietly as the men on board the three ships did. In a few minutes, they emerge with the cart loaded with coffee. Elizabeth Harrison stops beside Boylston who's still sitting on the ground.

ELIZABETH HARRISON: You're the one pretending to be king, Mr. Boylston. Charging such high prices. Expecting us to make you a rich man.

THOMAS BOYLSTON (*shouting*): I hope my coffee keeps you awake all night long! You'll have plenty to think about and be sorry for! (*muttering to himself*) A man can't even try to make a good living for himself and his family. (*appealing to Hancock*) You're a rich man. You know what I'm talking about. I haven't done anything wrong.

JOHN HANCOCK (*approaching and holding out his hand to help Boylston stand up*): The women of Boston seem to think you have done something wrong. I wouldn't go against them.

HONOR TURNER (*holding out the keys*): Your keys, Mr. Boylston. It was a pleasure doing business with you.

(Boylston ignores Hancock's outstretched hand. As the women leave, he's left behind, sitting on the ground.)

NARRATOR: The name for the harsh British rules stuck. But the Intolerable Acts backfired on the British. The acts united the American colonies. Food and supplies flowed into Boston. Virginia called for a Continental Congress. Representatives from every colony met in Philadelphia in the fall of 1774 to talk about what was happening in Boston. Committees of correspondence sprang up. The committees of each colony reported about British actions in its area and how its colonists were responding. Alarmed, the British sent more troops to Boston. A year later, the first shots in the American Revolution were fired.

What Happened?

The Boston Tea Party was a catalyst in bringing the colonies and England to war. The Tea Tax was only one in a series of taxes the British had levied on the colonies. England had won the French and Indian War and was the dominant foreign power in America, but the war had cost a great deal of money. One way to fill the British treasury was to collect duties and tariffs, the taxes placed on goods sent to and from the colonies. Because there were few factories in the colonies, raw materials were shipped to English factories, and manufactured products were sent to the colonies.

In 1764, England passed the Sugar Act. All cargo going in and out of the colonies had to be carried on British- or colony-owned ships. All tariffs and duties were to be strictly enforced. Customs houses were established. The British navy had the right to seize ships and their cargo and then auction them off. Since the colonies had no representation in the houses of Parliament, many colonists protested that the Sugar Act was taxation without representation.

Then, in 1765, England pressed the Stamp Act upon the colonies. All newspapers, bills of sale, legal documents, ads, pamphlets, and other documents had to have stamps on them, which cost money. The colonists were outraged. The Boston branch of the Sons of Liberty, a radical group, started a "committee of correspondence" with the other colonies to organize a protest against the latest example of taxation without representation. The colonies decided to boycott British goods. That action led to the repeal of the act. But another act, the Townshend Act, appeared in 1767. Lead, glass, paint, paper, and tea were taxed. This act, too, was repealed but replaced by a new act—the Tea Act of 1773. Tea was taxed, and only one company—the East India Company—could bring tea into the colonies, and only government-licensed merchants could sell it. The Boston Tea Party was the colonists' response. In retaliation, the British passed what the colonists called the Intolerable Acts.

The harsh new sets of laws sparked the first Continental Congress, which unified the colonies. In 1775, the first shots of the American Revolution were fired outside of Boston at the battles of Lexington and Concord.

📖 Read All About It!

Fritz, Jean. *Why Don't You Get a Horse,* Sam Adams? New York: Coward-McCann Inc., 1982.
Forbes, Esther. *Johnny Tremain*. New York: Dell Publishing, 1971.
Meltzer, Milton. *The American Revolutionaries: A History in Their Own Words 1750-1800*.
 New York: Thomas Y. Crowell, 1987.

📖 Read Some More!

Brenner, Barbara. *If You Were There in 1776*. New York: Bradbury Press, 1994.
Cohen, Amy. *From Sea to Shining Sea: A Treasury of American Folklore and Folk Songs*.
 New York: Scholastic, Inc., 1993.
Sherrow, Victoria. *Phillis Wheatley: Poet*. New York: Chelsea House, 1992.

ACTIVITIES

No Tea for Me!

Divide the class into two groups: the British and the colonists. Hold discussions about the Tea Tax. Were the groups able to come to a compromise? Would your groups have been able to stop the Boston Tea Party from happening? If so, how would that have changed the course of American history?

Right or Wrong?

The men and women of Boston took matters into their own hands. Both groups broke the law: the men trespassed on British ships and then dumped their cargo; the women forced a merchant to open his warehouse and then took his coffee. Ask your students to consider the following questions: Why do we consider these people as heroes and heroines rather than criminals? Is it ever right to break the law?

Eyewitness News

What if television had been invented in 1773? Let TV reporters prepare a news story about one of the events described in the play. Have them choose one scene. As they deliver their reports, classmates should re-enact the scene's action in the background. If possible, use a video camera to record the reports. You may expand the activity by holding a news talk show where a group of reporters discusses the events they covered and what the consequences of them may be.

I Protest!

Suppose your students were shop owners in Boston in the year 1773. Tea is one of their best-selling products. Then the Tea Act is passed. But the British won't give any of them a license to sell tea. What would they do? Would they write an editorial (or draw a political cartoon) for the newspaper or a letter to King George III? Would they make up a poem or a song about the unfair tax? Would they print a pamphlet that says the English should be thrown out of America? Encourage them to pick up pens and paper, and make their voices heard in England

A Taxing Project

The people of Boston were tea drinkers. The tax on tea was only a few pennies per pound. What difference does a few cents make? For this group project, students should find out which drinks are the most popular in their school cafeteria. Ask them to consider these questions: About how many of each drink are sold every day? About how many are sold during the school year? How many of those drinks do they estimate that they, personally, will buy during the school year? What if a tax of 5¢ were placed on every bottle, glass, or container of these drinks? How much tax money would be collected during the school year? How much in taxes would they end up paying?

1773: What a Year!

The city of Boston in 1773 was different than it is today. Was your town or city established by 1773? If so, what kind of government did it have? What did the community look like? If not, what was the landscape like? Who lived in the area? What kinds of plants and animals inhabited the area? As a class project, guide students in finding out how your community and its environment has changed since 1773. Encourage them to include drawings and/or models in their reports. Share their discoveries with other classes.

1838-1839
The Trail of Tears:
Nunna-da-ul-tsun-yi, The Place Where We Cried

By Sarah Glasscock

Characters (in order of appearance):

OLD SETTLER NARRATOR (from first group of Cherokee to move west)

RETURN J. MEIGS: U.S. government agent to Cherokee

JANE KINGFISHER: Cherokee Old Settler

ELIAS BOUDINOT: Editor of the *Cherokee Phoenix*

JOHN ROSS: Planter and president of the Cherokee nation

TREATY PARTY NARRATOR (from second group to move west)

MAJOR RIDGE: Founder of Treaty Party

NATIONAL PARTY NARRATOR (from last group to move west)

QUATIE ROSS: John Ross's wife

PAULA BLACKFOX: Cherokee woman

CHEROKEE GIRL (nonspeaking role)

ACT 1

Scene 1: 1803. At the U.S. government model farm on Cherokee land in what is now Georgia.

OLD SETTLER NARRATOR: In 1801, the United States government sent Return J. Meigs onto our lands. He brought plows for the men and looms for the women. He said we should give up hunting and become farmers. He said we should send our children to schools where they would learn to read and write English. We would become "civilized." But not everyone wanted to become civilized.

JANE KINGFISHER: I'm returning your loom, Mr. Meigs.

RETURN J. MEIGS: But why? You make such beautiful cloth.

JANE KINGFISHER: It's not as soft as deer cloth. It doesn't last as long. My husband's returning the plow, also. He's a hunter, not a farmer.

RETURN J. MEIGS: He was a hunter. Now, he must become a farmer. If you grow your own crops, you'll never be hungry. There aren't as many deer as there were—

JANE KINGFISHER: Because you've let white people move onto our hunting grounds. You think that if we don't hunt, we don't have any use for our land. You think that if we don't have any use for our land, that you white people should have it.

RETURN J. MEIGS: The white people aren't going to go away, Jane. You know that. You have to change. You have to learn how to live like us.

JANE KINGFISHER: What if we don't?

RETURN J. MEIGS: Then you can move west. President Jefferson says that you can go live on the land we just got from France. You can keep your traditions.

JANE KINGFISHER: Why should we move? Why should we change? This is our home, not yours.

RETURN J. MEIGS: White and Cherokee—we all live here now.

JANE KINGFISHER: But soon only whites will live here.

RETURN J. MEIGS: It's up to you, Jane. Either change or move west.

OLD SETTLER NARRATOR: Jane and her family moved west into what is now northeastern Texas. Other Cherokee followed and settled in parts of Arkansas and Texas. Those who left the east were called the Old Settlers. Not all of us moved west because we wanted to keep our traditional ways. Some of us wanted to explore the economic opportunities in the new territory.

Scene 2: 1831. In the office of the Cherokee Phoenix newspaper.

TREATY PARTY NARRATOR: Fewer Cherokee migrated west than the government had hoped. Removal was the government's name for the move. Many of us who stayed in the East became successful planters. In many ways, the "civilization" program worked. But, still, white settlers continued to move onto our territory. The land was rich and good for growing cotton. In 1819, we, the eastern Cherokee, voted to stop ceding, or giving away, any more of our land. In 1827, we wrote our own constitution. By 1819, Sequoyah had developed a Cherokee alphabet, so we were able to read and write in our own language. In 1828, Elias Boudinot established a newspaper, the Cherokee Phoenix. Oh, by the way, in that same year, gold was discovered in Georgia—some was found on Cherokee land.

ELIAS BOUDINOT: I hate printing news like this.

JOHN ROSS: It's only a setback. We'll keep fighting.

ELIAS BOUDINOT: A setback?! The Supreme Court's just ruled that the Cherokee nation is not an independent nation. It's okay that Georgia's outlawed our government. It's okay that we can't testify in their courts against white men. It's okay that we can't even mine gold on our own lands. It's not our gold. It's white gold.

JOHN ROSS: We have a good, legal claim to this land. We've lived on it for hundreds of years. We were here long before the state of Georgia was. We've got friends in Washington, D.C.

ELIAS BOUDINOT: Who? Andrew Jackson? President Andrew Jackson who just made sure the Indian Removal Act got passed? He'll have us paddling across the Mississippi River before you know it.

JOHN ROSS: No, he's no friend to us, but he's not the only man in Washington. Look at your desk. You've got a stack of newspaper editorials from Maine to Virginia supporting us. We've got Sam Houston and Daniel Webster with us. Jackson can't go against them and the American people.

ELIAS BOUDINOT: Who's going to tell Jackson that? You?

NATIONAL PARTY NARRATOR: The next year the Supreme Court ruled that Georgia law didn't apply to the Cherokee. That meant we had the right to create our own form of government. We had control of our own land.

ACT 2

Scene: March 1835. At Major Ridge's plantation in the Coosa Valley.

TREATY PARTY NARRATOR: Too bad that the state of Georgia ignored the Supreme Court ruling. Too bad that Andrew Jackson said, "John Marshall [Chief Justice of the

Supreme Court] has made his decision, now let him enforce it." Boudinot, along with his uncle Major Ridge and Ridge's son John, formed the Treaty Party. Those of us who joined saw that it was useless to fight. It was better to sell our land to the government and move west.

NATIONAL PARTY NARRATOR: In 1835, the Treaty Party sold out the Cherokee people. One hundred Treaty Party members made a deal with Washington. In exchange for five million dollars, they agreed to give up all Cherokee land in the East and move west. Too bad they didn't ask the rest of us—15,000 of us—what we wanted to do. We signed a petition of protest against the treaty, and John Ross got ready to take the 15,000 signatures to Washington.

MAJOR RIDGE: And what if we hadn't signed the treaty? What do you think would happen to us? One way or the other, they're going to take our land. At least we got the government to pay us something. You and your petition. What good will that do? Wave your pieces of paper under those senators' noses. Will they care? No! We were right to get what we could out of them!

JOHN ROSS: You signed the treaty because it was good for you. You weren't thinking about the Cherokee people. You were thinking about power and money. Well, you got what you wanted. How does it feel?

MAJOR RIDGE: I'll see you in the West, John Ross. I hope you make it before the best land is gone.

TREATY PARTY NARRATOR: Major Ridge had fought beside Andrew Jackson in the War of 1812. He knew what kind of man the president was. John Ross and his petition didn't mean anything. By one vote, the United States Senate ratified the treaty. They gave us two years to make the move west. About 2,000 of us left immediately.

OLD SETTLER NARRATOR: Believe me—we weren't exactly thrilled to see the Treaty Party move in. We were settled. We had our own ways. Then we heard that 13,000 more were due in two years.

TREATY PARTY NARRATOR: And what did John Ross and the rest of you do? Nothing. You stayed. You made no plans. And what happened?

NATIONAL PARTY NARRATOR: The U.S. Army moved into the Cherokee Nation. They took our rifles and guns. White settlers began to take our land.

 **ACT 3**

Scene: January 1839. Aboard the steamboat Victoria. January 1839.

OLD SETTLER NARRATOR: You could have come west a long time ago.

TREATY PARTY NARRATOR: You could have gotten money and land. You could have come with us.

NATIONAL PARTY NARRATOR: No, we couldn't. We were in the right. The treaty was no good. But in the fall of 1837, President Martin Van Buren told the U.S. Army to round us up. It was harvest time. We were forced to leave the crops rotting in the fields. We only had enough time to collect a few things from our homes. We were locked up in stockades. That winter was very harsh. We had little food. We ran out of firewood. Many of us died. In the spring, we were told we had to march to Arkansas. They sent about 5,000 of us in the first group. We got spoiled food. Many more died. At John Ross's request, Washington stopped the move until cooler weather in the fall. He also received permission to let us handle the removal ourselves.

OLD SETTLER NARRATOR: You only have yourselves to blame.

TREATY PARTY NARRATOR: We warned you. If John Ross had listened to Major Ridge, his wife Quatie might not have died. She might not have been on that boat, trying to help the sick.

QUATIE ROSS: It won't be long now. We've almost reached Little Rock. Then we'll go up to Fort Smith. After that, it's only 50 miles by wagon to Fort Gibson.

PAULA BLACKFOX: I better not see that Major Ridge when I get there. He won't be standing on top of the ground for long.

QUATIE ROSS: He was wrong to do what he did. But we can't fight each other. That won't do anybody any good.

PAULA BLACKFOX: You know he and his son and Elias Boudinot have already taken the best land. What will the rest of us do?

QUATIE ROSS: What we've always done. We'll learn, and we'll survive.

PAULA BLACKFOX (*pointing across the deck to a small girl who's shivering*): If we survive. (*Quatie Ross hurries across the deck to the small girl. She takes off her own coat and wraps it around the girl. Paula Blackfox follows her.*) You'll freeze.

QUATIE ROSS (*laughing*): No, I won't. You'll just have to stand in front of me and keep the wind away.

PAULA BLACKFOX (*pulling her dress away from her waist*): Are you kidding? Look how much weight I've lost since we left. I couldn't even keep a little breeze away. You spend too much time around these sick people. Let their families take care of them.

QUATIE ROSS: But their families are sick. They need someone to look after them.

PAULA BLACKFOX: You don't have to do all these things just because your husband's the chief.

QUATIE ROSS: It's easier if I'm busy. I think too much about the past and the future if I'm not doing something.

NATIONAL PARTY NARRATOR: Quatie Ross became ill and died before the Victoria landed in Little Rock. It's estimated that between one-fourth and one-half of the Cherokee population died on the trail west. That's why we call the move Nunna-da-ul-tsun-yi, the place where we cried. Some call it the Trail of Tears.

OLD SETTLER NARRATOR: You should have come with us.

TREATY PARTY NARRATOR: You should have come with us.

What Happened?

When they first came in contact with Europeans in 1540, the Cherokee occupied portions of the present-day states of Kentucky, West Virginia, Virginia, North and South Carolina, Georgia, and Alabama. That first encounter was disastrous. Hernando de Soto was in search of gold, which he didn't find. He and his men murdered many Cherokee and killed others through the spread of diseases: such as measles, smallpox, and the bubonic plague. The second encounters with Europeans—the English in the 1700s—was more positive. A trading relationships grew between the two groups: the Cherokee traded deerskins for metal farming tools. Although the Cherokee supported the English in the French and Indian War, the English took over Cherokee hunting land after the war. Then came the American Revolution. The Cherokee aided the British and paid for it by having to give up a large amount of land to the United States.

The new country of America tried several approaches in dealing with the Cherokee (as well as other Native American groups). In the late 1700s, an attempt was made to "civilize" the Cherokee, or assimilate them into white society. At about the same time, a movement known as removal was introduced by President Thomas Jefferson. He suggested that Native Americans abandon their homes in the East and move west of the Mississippi to the newly acquired territory of the Louisiana Purchase (despite the fact that the land was already occupied). A group of Cherokee, the Old Settlers, took up the offer. It was a mixed group of traditionalists, pioneers, and people anxious to get away from enemies. Those who remained in the East were encouraged to farm rather than hunt; missionaries moved into their settlements and set up schools. The Cherokee began to make the transition: They became successful planters; their children learned to read and write; a syllabary was created for their native language.

Their progress alarmed many white settlers. In 1827, the Cherokee drafted a constitution which set up a republic and also delineated their territory. The states in which this territory was located ignored the constitution. After the discovery of gold, Georgia, especially, refused to recognize the rights of the Cherokee. The Cherokee took a case against the state to the Supreme Court twice. Georgia won the first case, but lost the second, which meant that the state had to recognize Cherokee independence. The state refused to do so. A small group of Cherokee, known as the Treaty Party, secretly negotiated a treaty with the U.S. government. The majority of the Cherokee were outraged by the treaty and petitioned Washington to put a stop to it. The petition was ignored. The Cherokee were given two years in which to move west.

When the two years were up and the Cherokee showed no inclination to leave, federal troops under Winfield Scott moved into the territory in the summer of 1838. People were rounded up and put into stockades, and then they were shipped west. After disastrous losses of life, Chief John Ross asked the government if he could take over the removal. The government agreed. That winter, the majority of the Cherokee people began to move west. Of the 19,000 people who were forced to move west, about 2,500 died in the first roundup and in the stockades and about 1,500 died on the journey. In the West, the survivors formed the National Party.

📖 Read All About It!

Banks, Sara H. *Remember My Name*. Niwot, CO: Roberts Rinehart Publishers, 1993.
Meyers, Madeline. *Cherokee Nation: Life Before the Tears*. Lowell, MA: Discovery Enterprises, 1993.
Underwood, Tom. *Cherokee Legends and the Trail of Tears*. Cherokee, NC: Cherokee Publications, 1956.

📖 Read Some More!

Hoyt-Goldsmith, Diane. *Cherokee Summer*. New York: Holiday House, 1993.
Mankiller, Wilma. *Mankiller: A Chief and Her People*. New York: St. Martin's Press, 1993.
Roop, Peter and Connie Roop. *Ahyoka and the Talking Leaves*. New York: Lothrop, Lee & Shepard, 1992.

ACTIVITIES

East or West?

With which group do students most identify: the Old Settlers who first traveled to Texas and Arkansas, the members of the Treaty Party who went west in 1835, or the majority who moved in 1838? Randomly divide the class into groups of three or four. Ask each member to share his or her decision with the other members and to explain their reasons. If there are different opinions within the groups, encourage students to try to talk the other members into joining them. As a whole, how does your class divide? Which group is more numerous? Which was most successful in converting members?

Once Upon a Time

Provide a variety of Cherokee folktales. Suggested sources are *Cherokee Animal Tales* edited by George Scheer and *How Rabbit Tricked Otter and Other Cherokee Trickster Tales* and *How Turtle's Back Was Cracked* both by Gayle Ross. Let students browse through the books to find folktales that they especially like. Ask them to read over the stories until they feel comfortable enough to retell the stories before the class. Let the students lead discussions about their chosen folktales. End the activity by moderating talk about the importance of folktales.

A New Language

Sequoyah created the syllabary for the Cherokee language. He assigned a character to each syllable of the language. Have students create their own syllabaries. They can use their syllabaries to write out messages to friends. First, they should divide the words into syllables, and then give each syllable its own special character. They can then rewrite the messages using their syllabaries. Students can pass their syllabaries and keys to the characters and let friends translate the messages.

Pros and Cons

Americans had mixed feelings about the removal of the Cherokee from their homes. There was sympathy and outrage in the North (although it was pointed out in the South that the Northerners didn't have to worry about Indian removal because they had pretty much destroyed all the native tribes in their states), while Georgians felt that they had a right to the Cherokee land. Encourage students to write editorials for a newspaper in Maine that blasts the action and then write editorials for a newspaper in Georgia that justifies the action.

Trail of Tears Routes

Present a map that shows the different routes the Cherokee people took from their homelands to the new territory west of the Mississippi River. Have groups of students research the routes and write reports on them. Their reports should consider the advantages and disadvantages of each route (climate and weather; terrain; types of transportation; availability of food, water, and shelter; mileage; possibility of attack; and so on).

Art: A Window to the Past

What has happened to the Cherokee people since the removal in 1838? Students may choose to give an overview of the years following the Trail of Tears, or they may research one person or event. Encourage them to expand their studies to the arts. For instance, how does the work of contemporary artists tell stories about the past? What does it say about life today? Remind students to consider all forms of art in their presentations (e.g., prose and poetry, and visual art including paintings, sculpture, beadwork, and basket making.)

1847
The Oregon Trail:
Westward Ho!
One Family's Journey

By Liza Charlesworth

Characters (in order of appearance):

NARRATOR

READER

APPLETON FAMILY:

GRAMMY

MA

PA

CADDIE: a 12-year-old girl

JEM: an 8-year-old boy

BABY SARAH: a 2-year-old girl

JUSTIN LESTER: the wagon train's trail guide

PIONEERS 1-3 (nonspeaking roles)

TALL GRASS WAVING: a Sioux man

SIOUX MEN 1-3 (nonspeaking roles)

ACT 1

Scene: 5 A.M., April 12, 1847. Independence, Missouri. A wagon train full of families heading west is getting ready to pull out.

NARRATOR: The famous Oregon Trail, which officially opened in 1843, was the single most important route west during the 19th century. The trail began in Independence, Missouri; snaked through what is now Kansas, Nebraska, Wyoming, and Idaho; then ended in Oregon City, Oregon. About half a million settlers made the journey—crossing a giant patchwork of lush plains, parched deserts, and rugged mountains—to begin new lives in the promising West. But the 2,000 mile, five-to-eight-month trek was far from easy. How do we know? A few of the people who traveled it left a record of their incredible adventures behind in the pages of their diaries.

READER: From Caddie's diary: April 11, 1847. *Dear Diary: Tomorrow morning Ma, Pa, Jem, Baby Sarah, and I are leaving for Oregon City. Pa says the land there is good for farming and the woods are full of all kinds of critters like we've never seen. And he promises that we can go to school, just like we do here. I'm excited, but I'm scared too. Independence is the only home I've ever known. We're traveling in a wagon train with lots of other people, so we won't be lonely. Pa painted our prairie schooner bright red and brushed the oxen. Ma dipped the schooner's canvas in linseed oil to help keep the rain out. Because the schooner's wagon is so much smaller than our house, we sold most of our things, included my fancy dolls. I'll miss them, but not as much as Grammy . . .*

JUSTIN LESTER (*approaching the Appletons*): Howdy, folks! I 'spect you know I'm Justin Lester, hired on as your official trail guide. We'll be headin' out soon. You and the other families'll make up the rear of the wagon train. Me and my boys will be out front watching for trouble.

JEM (*eyes widening*): Trouble?!

JUSTIN LESTER: Just the usual: quicksand, twisters, ragin' rivers, storms, locusts, wolves, rattlers—

JEM (*looking worried*): R-r-r-r-rattlesnakes?

JUSTIN LESTER: You bet! No need to worry, though. I know the Oregon Trail like the back of my hand.

(*He displays his filthy hand, smiles, and walks off to greet other pioneers.*)

MA: We can only hope that he knows what he's doing.

GRAMMY (*hugging the children*): I'm going to miss you all so much! (*handing each of them a peppermint stick*) Sweets for my sweets!

CADDIE: I love you, Grammy!

BABY SARAH: I wuv ooo, Gammy!

(As they all laugh at Baby Sarah, a bugle sounds.)

PA: That's our cue! We're off to the land of milk and honey!

(The family climbs into the prairie schooner.)

THE WHOLE FAMILY *(waving)*: Bye, Grammy! We'll miss you!

GRAMMY *(wiping her eyes with a hankie)*: Bye darlings . . . have a wonderful adventure!

 **ACT 2**

Scene: 5:30 P.M., April 19, 1847. A prairie, somewhere in what is now Kansas.

NARRATOR: The group of wagon trains, about 40 of them, have formed a circle. In the middle of it, a weak fire, tended by the women, burns. Their fuel is running low. The men, meanwhile, are out hunting for food. A buffalo herd was spotted, and they're chasing after it.

READER: From Caddie's diary: April 19, 1847. *Dear Dairy, We've been traveling a week now, but I swear we weren't more than a few hours outside Independence before Jem asked if we were there yet! Ma and Pa just laughed. Baby Sarah and Jem ate their peppermint sticks right away. But not me, I'm saving mine 'til I get to Oregon. That way, it will be like Grammy is with us. The trip is going slow and steady. We make 12 miles on a good day. A good day is when there isn't rain to slow us, mud to get stuck in, or rivers to cross. There are lots of strange new things to get used to, especially in the evening when our wagon train stops and makes camp . . .*

MA *(stoking the fire)*: That's the last of our wood. Jem, go fetch me a bucket of buffalo chips.

JEM: Yuck! Do I have to?

MA: Look around you: There's nothing else to burn, so we'll have to use chips. Now, scoot. Caddie, you mind Baby Sarah.

(Pa and a group of men return with guns slung over their shoulders, and some carry odd-looking birds.)

CADDIE: Pa! What happened to the buffalo?

PA: The herd moved on, but we got us somethin' better: A prairie chicken!

(He proudly displays the bird.)

CADDIE (*making a face*): A prairie chicken? What's that?

MA: Now, Caddie, we must be thankful for the food we're given. (*Looking skeptically at the bird*) With a few wild onions, some carrots, and . . . lots of spices . . . I'm sure it will make a fine stew.

PA: That's the pioneer spirit! Caddie, bring me my fiddle, and I'll play 'til supper!

ACT 3

Scene: 3:00 P.M., June 24, 1847. In the middle of what is now Nebraska. A group of tipis are visible against the horizon.

READER: From Caddie's diary: June 24, 1847. *Dear Diary: We have now traveled 850 miles. It rains and rains; Jem and I walk and walk. In fact, Ma's had to patch our shoes twice. Baby Sarah caught a fever shortly after a bad hail storm and Ma's been tending her since: keeping her cool with rags dipped in water, feeding her weak tea, and singing to her. Sometimes we pass wooden grave markers, showing where people have died of hunger or the cholera, which worries me some. But Ma says not to think that way: Our Baby Sarah will be up and around in no time. Way back in Independence, I picked a far-away star and named it Oregon City; it doesn't seem to be getting any closer. But every-day on the trail is a new adventure . . .*

NARRATOR: The wagon train bumps along the road, still muddy from recent rains. Men are driving the wagons, women and children are walking. All eyes are on the tipis in the distance . . . suddenly . . .

CADDIE: Look, Indians! And they're coming this way!

NARRATOR: Four Sioux men—wearing buffalo hides decorated with beads, feathers, and porcupine quills—ride toward the front of the wagon train. A few carry tomahawks.

JEM: Look, they have tomahawks! Maybe they want to steal our horses! Or our food! Or maybe they want to—

CADDIE: Oh hush up! Maybe they just want to trade.

(A bugle sounds and the wagon train stops dead.)

MA (*looking worried*): Children! Get inside the schooner! Now!

(Caddie and Jem scramble into the schooner. Jem pokes his head out the front to see what's happening.)

JEM: What kind of Indians are they, Pa?

PA: Sioux, I reckon.

CADDIE *(from inside the schooner, to Jem)*: What's going on out there?

JEM *(straining to see)*: Well, one Indian is talking and moving his hands around fast and furious. He looks upset. Now Justin Lester is talking and moving his hands around fast and furious. He looks real upset. Now Justin Lester and the Indians are coming this way—uh-oh!

PA: Jem, that's enough! Get back inside with your Ma and sisters.

(Justin Lester and Tall Grass Waving approach the wagon.)

JUSTIN LESTER: Folks, I don't mean to alarm you, but I got some unfortunate news.

JEM *(from inside the wagon)*: See? What'd I tell you? We're done for!

PA *(trying to ignore the voice coming out of the schooner)*: What seems to be the problem?

TALL GRASS WAVING: The creek ahead is full from the rains. You won't be able to cross it in your wagons.

JEM *(sounding surprised)*: I can understand what he's saying!

CADDIE: That's because he's speaking English.

PA *(surprised)*: But we have to cross the creek.

TALL GRASS WAVING: We can show you a place—about "a white man mile" from the trail where it's safe to cross.

PA: Thank you for helping us.

TALL GRASS WAVING: Someday, maybe you can help me.

PA: I hope so.

MA: What a good man . . . *(sighing and feeling Baby Sarah's hot forehead)* I hope this means our luck's changing.

ACT 4

Scene 1: 7:00 A.M., August 29, 1847. At the foot of the Cascade Mountains in what is now Oregon.

READER: From Caddie's diary: August 29, 1847. *Dear Diary: We have now traveled more than 1,900 miles. Only 100 more, but Oregon City still seems a million miles away. Our pretty red prairie schooner is now black with dirt. When I get to feeling gloomy, I remember my favorite day: The day we reached the Register of the Desert—this giant rock where hundreds of other pioneers have scratched their names and destinations. Most of those folks are probably in their new homes now. Today, I've only eaten one biscuit and a small piece of bacon. Food is low and we got to make sure Baby Sarah gets her fill. The good news is she seems to be a little better. Yesterday, she was well enough to sit up. Pa says we'll soon face our last challenge—climbing the Cascade Mountains . . .*

NARRATOR: Some wagons have already crossed the mountains, others are scattered at the base. Remembering what is was like to cross the Rockies, pioneers mill about nervously. This will be their last, and greatest, hurdle.

JUSTIN LESTER (*approaching the Appletons, then pointing up at a huge peak*): Do you think you're gonna make it over the mountain? Those oxen ain't lookin' too lively.

PA: They're hungry and tired, but they'll manage.

JUSTIN LESTER: The family gonna hike on up the foot path to lessen your load?

PA: Caddie and Jem will. But my wife has to ride in the wagon with Baby Sarah . . . she's still sick.

JUSTIN LESTER: I hope you know what you're doing. A lighter load 'n this one's been known to kill stronger beasts. They may have heart attacks.

PA: It's the only way. We can't turn back now.

JUSTIN LESTER: Make sure the children wear mittens, hats, and wraps, then. It's colder than a gooseberry in December up there. (*offering Pa a swig from his canteen*) And God speed, Appleton!

Scene 2: 2:00 P.M. at the top of the mountain.

NARRATOR: Caddie and Jem sit shivering on a rock, anxiously waiting for their parents.

JEM: What if they don't make it? What if the oxen die? What if—

CADDIE (*teeth chattering*): J-J-J-Jem Appleton, don't you talk that way. 'Course they'll make it!

JEM: C-C-C-Caddie! Here comes our wagon! I told you they'd make it!

PA (*speaking in a very tired voice*): Am I glad to see you! The wagon started to slip at Dead-Man's Pass, and I thought we were goners. But the oxen tugged and tugged, and we finally gained ground. I do believe they want to get to Oregon City as much as we do!

(*He hops down from the prairie schooner and hugs Jem and Caddie. Ma and Baby Sarah poke their heads out the back of the wagon.*)

CADDIE: Ma, Ma! I have a present for you, and one for Baby Sarah.

(*Caddie opens her hands to show two perfect snowballs.*)

MA: My word! Whoever heard of snowballs in August?

CADDIE: There's lots of snow under the trees!

BABY SARAH (*perking up and grabbing for her snowball*): Sow Poe! Sow Poe!

(*The family laughs.*)

MA: Look at the roses in Sarah's cheeks! I do declare, adventure agrees with her!

(*Pa points to the gorgeous green valley at the bottom of the western slope of the mountain.*)

PA: And just look down there!

JEM: What, Pa? I don't see anything.

PA (*proudly*): Our new home—at last!!

READER: From Caddie's diary: September 12, 1847. *Dear Diary: Well, we finally made it! 2,000 miles and 141 days later! I write to you from my new home, just a skip from Oregon City. Pa went to town today to buy some glass for the house he's building. We're going to have real windows, just like we used to! In a few days, Jem and I will start school in a brand-new school house, just a couple miles away.*

Baby Sarah, mercifully, is all better and quite a ball of fire, I might add. Yesterday, she got hold of my peppermint stick—remember the one from Grammy, that I toted all the way from Independence? Well, she chewed it right up! Speaking of Grammy, I wrote her a real long letter. Pa's mailing it in town today. If all goes well, Grammy will get it next summer. Then it will be almost like I'm talking to her, telling her all about our amazing adventure on the Oregon Trail.

What Happened?

In May of 1843, the first wagon train started down the Oregon Trail, and the rush west began. The 2,000-mile trail led from Independence, Missouri, to the fertile lands known as Oregon Country—about 500,000 square miles containing parts of what are now Nebraska, Wyoming, Idaho, California, Oregon, and Washington. A trip on the Oregon Trail was long and arduous, taking from five to eight months; the Conestoga wagons, or prairie schooners, averaged a sluggish 12 miles on a good day. So many forces conspired to curtail or end a pioneer's journey: tornadoes, quicksand, fires, early snowstorms, impassable rivers and mountains, cholera, malaria, starvation, and occasional Indian encounters. In all, the trail claimed the lives of 35,000 pioneers, or about 1/14th of the 500,000 who attempted it.

Although skirmishes with Native Americans groups have historically been cited as a primary obstacle, far more lives were lost to sickness than to attacks, and many tribes proved to be both invaluable guides and trading partners. Trouble began only when the pioneers settled on Native American land. The Oregon Trail had its beginnings years before white settlers arrived in America. Native Americans had forged paths through the difficult terrain; the Oregon Trail linked up hundreds of these paths. Lewis and Clark were the first non-Indian explorers to venture westward along this route. Solitary mountain men—such as James Bridger, Jim Beckwourth, and Kit Carson—soon followed, mostly making their living by trapping. Others, like John Jacob Astor, sailed to the Oregon country. Both Great Britain and the United States had laid claim to the Oregon Country. The influx of American pioneers helped settle the question of ownership.

Today, only about 15 percent of the original route remains. But in some spots you can still see the deep groves left behind by the wagon trains 140 years ago.

📖 Read All About It!

Gildemeister, Jerry. *A Letter Home. Union*, OR: Bear Wallow Publishing Co., 1987.
Parkman, Frances. *Oregon Trail*. New York: Airmont, 1964.
Place, Marian T. *Westward on the Oregon Trail*. New York: American Heritage Junior Library, 1962.
Stickney, Joy. *Native Americans along the Oregon Trail*. Husun, WA: Canyon Creations, 1993.

📖 Read Some More!

Fleischman, Paul. *Townsend's Warbler*. New York: HarperCollins Publishers, 1992.
Freedman, Russell. *Children of the Wild West*. New York: Clarion Books, 1983.
Levine, Ellen. *If You Traveled West in a Covered Wagon*. New York: Scholastic, 1986.

ACTIVITIES

Pioneers Past and Present

What does it really mean to be a pioneer? Which of these words best describes a pioneer: brave, determined, the first? Guide your students in compiling a list of words to define what a pioneer is, and then have them list individuals who they feel fit their descriptions. Can your students think of any ways in which they are pioneers?

To Be or Not to Be . . . a Pioneer

Why did some families, like the Appletons, decide to go West, while others choose to stay put in Boston or Philadelphia or rural New York state? Discuss the very real pros and cons of traveling on the Oregon Trail in 1847. Then take a class tally to find out who would have undertaken the journey and who would have remained in the east. Encourage students to share their reasons with the rest of the class.

Dear Diary

Some of the pioneers who journeyed on the Oregon Trail kept track of their exciting trips by recording what happened. The diary entries in "Westward Ho!" are written by a fictional 12-year-old named Caddie Appleton. What other adventures might Caddie have had: A close encounter of the rattlesnake kind, a new friend at Fort Laramie, a tornado dancing across the plains? After students have dipped into some of the books contained in the bibliography, have them write one or more new entries in Caddie's diary. If they wish, students may create more scenes for the play, too!

Trail Tall Tales

To entertain themselves after a long day of travel, pioneers often told stories around a campfire. Some of the tales were scary and had been passed down from generation to generation; others were funny and invented on the spot. Let individuals or groups decide upon their own favorite stories to retell. Then, turn the lights down low, and share the stories around a pretend "classroom campfire." For a finale, create a classroom story. Begin the tale with a sentence such as, "It was a dark and stormy night on the plains . . . ." Going clockwise around the circle, each student contributes one more sentence to build the story. If possible, use a cassette player to record the story.

The Great Plains Then and Now

The Oregon Trail was a study in contrasts. It crossed gentle prairies, deserts, majestic mountains; skirted Indian villages, awesome rock formations, and crowded forts. Challenge students to find out more about the key landmarks on the trail. What were they like in the 1840s when families like the Appletons encountered them? What are they like today? The research material can be presented in the form of past and present travel brochures. Traveling from east to west, have students present their brochures in order. Incorporate the students' work into a mural map of the trail.

Take a Left at Fort Laramie

The Appletons left Independence, Missouri, in April and arrived in Oregon City in September. Today, if you flew, that same trip might take only a day. During the recent anniversary of the Oregon Trail, some people rode in wagons and on horseback to retrace the steps of the pioneers. What form(s) of transportation would your students use to travel from Independence to Oregon City? Have them create a travel plan that includes type of transportation, a complete itinerary, estimated timetable of arrivals and departures, and estimated mileage. About how much will their trip cost? (Remind everyone to consider transportation, food, lodging, souvenirs, and unexpected costs.)

Women's Rights Conventions:
Ain't I a Woman?

By Sarah Glasscock

Characters (in order of appearance):

NARRATOR

ELIZABETH CADY STANTON: Feminist and organizer of 1848 convention in Seneca Falls, NY (*A feminist is someone who supports women's rights.*)

STANTON'S NEPHEW

LUCRETIA COFFIN MOTT: Feminist and organizer of 1848 convention in Seneca Falls, NY

WILLIAM LLOYD GARRISON: Feminist and abolitionist

WOMAN 1

MAN 1

FREDERICK DOUGLASS: Feminist and abolitionist (*An abolitionist is someone who fights against slavery.*)

MEN HECKLERS 1-2

WOMEN HECKLERS 1-2

FRANCES GAGE: Feminist and chair of 1851 convention in Akron, OH

SOJOURNER TRUTH: Feminist and abolitionist

ACT 1

Scene 1: Morning of July 19, 1848. Outside locked church in Seneca Falls, NY. A crowd is gathered.

NARRATOR: Lucretia Mott, a Quaker minister, and Elizabeth Cady Stanton began their plans for a women's rights convention in London. They were there to attend the World Anti-Slavery Convention. But at this abolition convention, women weren't allowed to speak or be seated as members. The two women decided a convention needed to be held to talk about the "social, civil, and religious rights of women." Eight years later, the convention is about to begin at a church—only the church is locked.

STANTON (*speaking through open window*): Are you all right?

NEPHEW (*from inside church*): Yep. Piece of cake.

STANTON: Good. Unlock the door, and I'll give you all the cake you want.

NEPHEW: Promise?

STANTON: On my honor.

MOTT (*breaking through crowd*): Elizabeth! They can't find the key anywhere! I can't believe it!

STANTON: What? The lost key or the crowd?

MOTT: Both! Hundreds of people are waiting in the hot sun. This doesn't look good. This doesn't look good at all. The church should be unlocked. Everyone should be sitting down. I can just see the newspapers now: How can Elizabeth Stanton and Lucretia Mott say that women should have the same rights as men? They hold a convention for women's rights—only nobody can get into the building where it's supposed to be held!

STANTON: Don't worry. My nephew's saved the day. He'll let us in.

MOTT: I just wish you had a niece instead of a nephew. I'd rather have a female saving the day.

NEPHEW: I heard that!

STANTON: It's nothing personal.

NEPHEW: I don't know. It sounds like she wants to take away my rights.

STANTON: Now, you know better than that. We don't want to take away anybody's rights. We'd just like some of our own, thank you very much.

(The church door swings open.)

NEPHEW *(from behind the door)*: So long as I don't have to cook and clean and take care of babies.

STANTON *(entering church)*: Haven't you heard? That's the easy work.

Scene 2: Evening of that day. Inside the empty church.

NARRATOR: That first day, a Declaration of Rights and Sentiments was signed by 68 women and 32 men. This declaration of women's equality was based on the Declaration of Independence. "We hold these truths to be self-evident; that all men and women are created equal; that they are endowed by their Creator with certain inalienable rights; that among these are life, liberty, and the pursuit of happiness; that to secure these rights governments are instituted, deriving their just powers from the consent of the governed." On the second day of the convention, a list of resolutions would be read and voted upon.

STANTON: There must have been 300 people at the meeting today, and we just put that one little notice in the Seneca Falls newspaper. Think if we had advertised in a New York City paper, or one in Boston!

MOTT: We're off to a good start. *(holding up the Declaration)* It's too bad Thomas Jefferson and the rest of the founding fathers left so many of us out of the Constitution.

STANTON: It is a good start. And tomorrow we vote on the resolutions.

MOTT *(slowly putting down the Declaration)*: Elizabeth—I want to talk to you about one of the resolutions.

STANTON *(pretending to be surprised)*: Oh? Which one? That any law that works against the "true and substantial happiness of women" is no law at all?

MOTT: No—

STANTON: Then is it the one that says no laws should prevent women from "occupying such a station in society as her conscience shall dictate" or make her inferior to men?

MOTT: You know which one I'm—

STANTON: Then it must be the resolution that clearly states that woman is the equal of man. Resolution nine, my favorite.

MOTT: It's the question of the vote. It's too early to present that. We'll have to work up to it. We can't do, or undo, everything in one convention.

STANTON: How can we change any laws if we can't vote? How can the President speak for us, or any man in the Senate or the House of Representatives speak for us, if they have not received our votes? We can't hold public office. We can't serve on juries. As married women, we aren't allowed to take care of our own money and property. If we divorce, our children are taken away from us.

MOTT: I know what women can and cannot do, Elizabeth. All right, you want women to have the vote? Well, we will tomorrow when we vote on the resolutions. What if your favorite resolution doesn't get passed? What if the women of the convention vote against the right to vote?

STANTON: I'm not afraid of women having the vote. I'm afraid of them not having it.

MOTT (*exasperated*): I'm not against the vote for women. You know that. I just think it's too early to discuss it. We'll lose more support than we'll gain.

STANTON: Then it's better to let people know where we stand right now. If they don't believe in giving women the right to vote, then how can they believe that we deserve any other rights?

MOTT: All right! We'll put resolution nine up for vote tomorrow. But be prepared. It may not pass.

STANTON: It will—you'll see.

Scene 3: July 20, 1848. Inside the crowded church.

NARRATOR: The next day the convention quickly got down to business. When we join the convention, eight resolutions have been voted on. All eight have passed unanimously—not one, single person in the church has voted against any of them. But now, Elizabeth Cady Stanton is about to read her favorite resolution, resolution number nine calling for the right of women to vote. The upcoming vote is making the crowd restless. They begin to talk and argue among themselves.

STANTON: Ladies and gentlemen—ladies and gentlemen!—it's now time to vote on resolution number nine. We are asking that women be given the right to vote. Ladies, you've been voting on resolutions all day long. How does it feel to have that power?

GARRISON (*rising*): Excuse me, Mrs. Stanton, but I believe it's a mistake to include this resolution with the others. We'll look ridiculous to the rest of the world.

STANTON: Ridiculous!? Why?

GARRISON: We are asking for too much, too fast. Women need to prepare themselves.

STANTON: Did George Washington need time to prepare himself to vote? Did Thomas Jefferson?

GARRISON (*wagging his finger at Elizabeth*): Now, Mrs. Stanton, that's different.

STANTON: Indeed? How is it different?

WOMAN 1: Forget about the vote! Move on to the next resolution!

MAN 1: I second that!

MOTT (*whispering to Douglass*): Mr. Garrison's right. If we pass the resolution, we will look ridiculous. If we don't pass the resolution, it's Elizabeth who'll look ridiculous.

DOUGLASS: There are worse things than looking ridiculous. (*rising to join Stanton and Garrison*) Mrs. Stanton, Mr. Garrison, if you'll allow me?

GARRISON: Good! Explain the situation to her, Mr. Douglass.

STANTON: Yes, please do explain.

DOUGLASS (*addressing the crowd*): Ladies—do not be fooled. You may be told that you need to be taught to learn how to vote. You may be told that having the vote will not change your lives. You may be told that you will never get the vote because you cannot make up your minds. You are not smart enough. You shouldn't worry your heads about making such hard choices. You cannot make such hard choices.

I was born a black man. I've had to make hard choices from the day I was born. You were born women. Think of the choices you've had to make in your own lives. Think of the choices that have been taken away from you. I don't want to be a white man. I'm pretty sure that none of the women here want to be white men. (No offense to Mr. Garrison.) But we want the same rights that white men have. That's why we're here. That includes having the right to vote. We will get nowhere without it. (*About half of the audience applauds his speech.*) Mrs. Stanton, would you read the resolution so we may vote on it?

STANTON: Thank you, Mr. Douglass. (*reading from the list of resolutions*) "Resolved: That it is the duty of the women of this country to secure to themselves their sacred right to the elective franchise." All in favor, raise your hands.

(*Stanton and Douglass raise their hands, along with some members of the audience. They count silently along with Garrison and Mott. They all nod in agreement at their numbers.*)

All right, all against, raise your hands.

(Mott and Garrison raise their hands, along with some members of the audience. Again, Stanton, Garrison, Mott, and Douglass count silently.)

STANTON (*smiling to the crowd*): The ayes have it! It is our duty to secure the vote!

GARRISON (*to Mott*): But it passed by such a narrow margin.

MOTT (*to Garrison*): A very narrow margin.

DOUGLASS (*overhearing them*): You call it a narrow margin. I call it a majority.

STANTON: Now, on to resolution number ten. "Resolved, That the equality of human rights results necessarily from the fact of the sameness of the race in capabilities and responsibilities." I believe Mr. Douglass has just proved that point.

NARRATOR: The first women's rights convention ended the next day. Many people made fun of the convention and what had been accomplished. Some of the signers of the Declaration took their names off of it. But other women's rights conventions were held. In Worcester, Massachusetts, in the fall of 1850, the first national convention attracted 1,000 people from 11 states. The convention's motto was "Equality before the law without distinction [regard or notice] of sex or color."

One of the speakers at the national convention in Massachusetts was Sojourner Truth. After hearing women talk on subjects ranging from wearing bloomers to receiving equal pay, Truth said, "Sisters, I'm not clear what you're after. If women want any rights more than they've got, why don't they just take them and not be talking about it."

ACT 2

Scene: 1851. Church in Akron, Ohio, where a women's rights convention is being held.

NARRATOR: Born into slavery but now a free woman, Sojourner Truth wanted to hear and talk about the hard problems that women faced. She also spoke at abolitionist conventions, too. Some people worried that Sojourner's stand on abolition would hurt the women's rights cause. People who might support women's rights would be turned off by her anti-slavery talk. But Sojourner continued to speak out on both issues. She traveled to Ohio, a free state with a large population of pro-slavery people. The crowds were often unfriendly, and her life was sometimes in danger. But this didn't stop Sojourner from going to a women's rights convention in Akron.

MAN HECKLER 1: God-fearing women! Leave this place now!

WOMAN HECKLER 1: Oh, shut up and leave yourself!

GAGE (*pounding a gavel*): Ladies and gentlemen! Please! Our next speaker is—

WOMAN HECKLER 2: You women should all be ashamed of yourselves! Go on home and take care of your families!

MAN HECKLER 2 (*jumping up*): That's right! That's why God created you!

(*Suddenly, the front door flies open. Sojourner Truth stands in the doorway. People recognize her and begin to whisper her name. She ignores them and walks to the only place left to sit—some steps at the front of the church.*)

GAGE (*smiling at Sojourner*): Welcome. (*The room is in an uproar; people are talking and pointing to the front of the church.*) I think we'll take a short break. We'll meet back here in fifteen minutes.

(*Gage steps toward Sojourner Truth to say hello, but several women stop her.*)

WOMAN 1: You can't let her speak!

WOMAN 2: She'll bring up slavery, you know she will.

WOMAN 3: Mrs. Smith says she'll leave if Sojourner Truth gets up to speak. She'll take Mrs. Bruce and Mrs. Adams with her, too.

WOMAN 4: We can't have a black woman address the convention. Not here in Ohio. There is no way—

GAGE: Ladies—we'll see when the time comes.

NARRATOR: Frances Gage leaves the church, and the four women trail after her. Shaking her head, Sojourner Truth watches them leave. In a few minutes, the church begins to fill up again. Gage returns to the front of the church. Sojourner rises.

MAN HECKLER 1: No! Don't let her speak!

WOMAN HECKLER 2: We don't need a slave coming in here and telling us what to do!

WOMAN HECKLER 1: Oh, shut up and sit down!

GAGE (*hesitating as Sojourner approaches*): Sojourner Truth.

TRUTH (*taking off her bonnet and looking out at the loud crowd until it quiets down*): Well, children, where there is so much racket, there must be something out of kilter . . . . But what's this all about anyway? (*pointing to a man in the audience*) That man over there. He says women need to be helped into carriages and lifted into ditches and to have the best everywhere. Nobody ever helps me into carriages, over mud puddles, or gets me any best places. And ain't I a woman? (pushing up the sleeve of her dress and then raising her right arm) Look at me! Look at my arm! I have plowed. And I have planted. And I have gathered into barns. And no man can head me. (whispering) And ain't I a woman? I could work as much and eat as much as a man—when I could get it—and bear the lash as well! And ain't I a woman? (pausing) I'm obliged to you for hearing me. And now old Sojourner hadn't got anything else to say.

(The crowd jumps to its feet, and the church is filled with the sound of clapping. Sojourner returns to her seat on the steps.)

NARRATOR: Elizabeth Cady Stanton, Lucretia Mott, Frederick Douglass, William Garrison, Frances Gage, and Sojourner Truth are only a few of the people who worked long and hard for women's rights. Although they all wanted to improve the role of women, they didn't always agree on the best way to do it. They argued and debated but still respected each other. Women didn't get the right to vote until 1919 when the Nineteenth Amendment was added to the Constitution.

What Happened?

Throughout its history, the women's rights movement has been closely associated with other movements, such as abolition, temperance, and civil rights. The first women's rights convention was organized by Elizabeth Cady Stanton and Lucretia Mott as a result of the treatment they'd received in 1840 at the World Anti-Slavery Convention. Held in London, that convention had refused to allow women to participate; women were free to observe the proceedings only. The convention in Seneca Falls demanded that women control their own property and wages, share custody of their children in cases of divorce, be able to speak freely and receive an education, pursue a profession—and the most controversial of all—be allowed to vote. Stanton's husband Henry threatened to leave town if she introduced the resolution to vote. She stuck by the resolution, and Henry left town. (He came back.)

As a result, other women's rights conventions were held. Lucy Stone, a gifted orator, and Susan B. Anthony, skilled at organization, became prominent in the movement. Both women were abolitionists, too. Stone had to agree to speak out on women's issues only on the weekends, while she devoted weekdays to the anti-slavery cause. During the Civil War and immediately afterward, the abolitionists wanted the emphasis on granting black men the vote, rather than women. But in 1869, the territory of Wyoming granted suffrage to its women citizens. In that same year, an amendment to the Constitution proposing women's suffrage was introduced in a joint resolution to Congress.

Susan B. Anthony was also active in the temperance movement, which came to prominence in the 1870s. Women had no legal protection against drunk husbands. Under the leadership of Frances Willard, the Women's Christian Temperance Union (WCTU) emphasized women's suffrage as a means for women to gain legal protection for themselves. This created a backlash; the liquor industry began to work against suffrage for women.

In the twentieth century, the work of Carrie Chapman Catt, Alice Paul, and Harriet Stanton Blatch (Elizabeth Cady Stanton's daughter) was instrumental in getting the Nineteenth Amendment passed, which granted women the right to vote.

📖 Read All About It!

Blumberg, Rhoda. *Bloomers!* New York: Bradbury Press, 1993.

Smith, Betsy Covington. *Women Win the Vote*. Englewood Cliffs, NJ: Silver Burdett Press, Inc., 1989.

Sullivan, George. *The Day the Women Got the Vote: A Photo History of the Women's Rights Movement*. New York: Scholastic Inc., 1994.

📖 Read Some More!

McKissack, Patricia C. and Frederick McKissack. *Sojourner Truth: Ain't I a Woman?* New York: Scholastic Inc., 1992.

Rappaport, Doreen. *American Women: Their Lives in Their Words*. New York: HarperTrophy, 1992.

ACTIVITIES

It's Got My Vote!

The headlines read "Fourth Graders Given the Vote!" The President has signed a bill that allows everyone in your class to vote in local, state, and national elections. How would your students use this right? With their new power, what would they try to change in the community, the state, and/or the country? Would some students sit out the elections, or certain elections? Discuss how having this new-found right might change their lives and the lives of other Americans.

What's the Difference?

One of the arguments that Sojourner Truth knocked down was that women were so physically weak they had to be "lifted over ditches." What limitations do the girls and boys in your classroom place on their own and the opposite gender? Are there some jobs that women or men shouldn't, or can't, do? Are there some rights and responsibilities that one gender should have but not the other? Throw out these questions to your class, and monitor the discussion.

Sorry—You're Wearing Blue

Ask students to write down one specific color that describes them, such as hair color, eye color, or the color of a piece of clothing they're wearing that day. Put their responses in a paper bag, and then draw one. After telling students what the description is, explain that anyone who fits that description can't participate in making any classroom decisions for the rest of the day. Have both groups, participants and non-participants, record their responses in journals. You may also wish to encourage the non-participants to group together to draw up a declaration of their rights and list of resolutions to present to the participants.

Voting for the First Time

Elected officials rely on the power of the vote. They keep their jobs, or lose them depending on the number of ballots cast. Prepare a list of local, state, and national elected officials who are women, and share it with your class. How did these women feel the first time they voted, or when they won their first elections? Let students choose one of the women to whom to write. If there are duplications, group students and have them write one letter. Post all responses on a bulletin board.

Changing Times

The Constitution was amended in 1919 to grant suffrage to women. Before that, several states had already given women that right. What led to these changes? Guide groups of students in researching the following topics: Alice Paul and Lucy Burns and their organization, the Congressional Union; the National Women Suffrage Association and Carrie Chapman Catt; Crystal Eastman and Jane Addams and the Women's International League for Peace and Freedom. Have groups then work together to weave their research into one class presentation.

Opening Doors

Along with the vote, many educational and professional opportunities were denied to women in the 1800s. Suggest that students create a timeline of "first women" for the classroom: the first woman doctor, the first woman in space, the first woman who was a self-made millionaire, and so on. Let students' own career and personal interests guide their research.

1863
Emancipation Proclamation:
Juneteenth

By Sarah Glasscock

Characters (in order of appearance):

JOELLE FERGUSON: 10 years old

C.J. FERGUSON: Joelle's twin

LANG FERGUSON: the twins' father

JILL FERGUSON: the twins' mother

MICHELLE HARPER: the twins' aunt

LORETTA FERGUSON: the twins' grandmother

JAMES FERGUSON: the twins' grandfather

ABRAHAM LINCOLN: 16th President of the United States

MARY TODD LINCOLN: First Lady

GENERAL GORDON GRANGER: Officer in the
    Union Army

ELLIS FERGUSON: the twins' great-great-great-great-
    grandfather (*10 years old in play*)

KING HAMILTON: Owner of large farm

ACT 1

Scene: June 19, 1995. The Ferguson family's Juneteenth celebration in a neighborhood park in Austin, Texas.

JOELLE: I want to be in the parade next year. I want to ride on a float and throw out candy.

C.J.: Not me. I want to march in the parade! Riding on a float—there's nothing to that.

MICHELLE: Do you two even know what we're celebrating today?

JOELLE AND C.J.: Juneteenth!

MICHELLE: And what is Juneteenth?

C.J.: June nineteenth.

MICHELLE: And what's so important about June nineteenth?

JOELLE: Every year on that day we have a parade and a barbecue and you come visit us.

MICHELLE (*to her sister-in-law Jill*): Aren't you teaching your children anything about anything?

JILL: They're teasing you. They know what today is.

JOELLE: It's when great-great-great-great-grandfather Ellis found out he didn't have to do what King Hamilton told him to do anymore.

JAMES: That's pretty close, but not exact. Let me tell you a story. Your great-great-great-great-grandfather Ellis (we'll just call him Ellis from now on) was on the Galveston docks when Major General Gordon Granger and his troops from the north sailed into the bay. The Civil War was over. Texas and the other southern states had surrendered. Now what? Nobody knew what was going to happen.

C.J.: Granger told everybody about the Emancipation Proclamation. He told the owners that they had to let us go free.

MICHELLE: As if we didn't already know about the Proclamation!

LORETTA: Oh my, yes, everybody knew. I remember all the stories my grandmother used to tell me. Abe Lincoln himself sent a messenger down with news of the Proclamation, but the messenger got killed. Or it took so long because the messenger was riding a mule, and you know how slow mules are. But we knew.

LANG: Just because there weren't any telephones or fax machines or computers with e-mail didn't mean that people didn't talk.

JAMES: As I was saying—Granger had landed. He told the crowd—blacks and whites—that he was here to make sure that the Emancipation Proclamation was enforced.

MICHELLE: Just because we didn't have our own clothes or homes or get paid for our work didn't mean we didn't talk. The owners tried to keep the Emancipation Proclamation a secret because they wanted to get one more crop into the ground. They couldn't do that without us helping them—for free—just like always.

ACT 2

Scene 1: September 22, 1862. The White House in Washington, D.C.

MARY TODD LINCOLN (*reading aloud from sheet of paper in her hand*): " . . . order and declare that all persons held as slaves within designated states and parts of states are, and henceforward shall be, free; . . . "

ABRAHAM LINCOLN: Well, Mary, what do you think? What does your southern blood say?

MARY TODD LINCOLN (*letting the paper rest in her lap*): So many people hate you so much already. Do you really have to do this? Can't you just say that slavery's wrong? (*pleading*) Oh, Abe, wait till the war's over to end slavery.

ABRAHAM LINCOLN: I'd do just about anything to end this war. I'd free all the slaves, I'd free some of them—I'd keep them in bondage forever if I thought that would bring peace to this country.

MARY TODD LINCOLN: Oh, Abe, you don't mean that.

ABRAHAM LINCOLN: I've never known anyone who wanted to be a slave. But I would trade places with one of Robert E. Lee's slaves if I thought it would end the war.

MARY TODD LINCOLN: I expect General Lee would think he got a bad deal if he saw you out in his fields.

ABRAHAM LINCOLN: Come January first of 1863, his fields will be empty. There won't be a black man, woman, or child working those fields. The owners won't be able to bring in their crops. Without food or any cash coming in, the southerners will have no choice. They'll have to surrender.

MARY TODD LINCOLN: But what's to become of them? Once they're free, where will they go?

ABRAHAM LINCOLN: We'll deal with that when we come to it.

Scene 2: June 19, 1865. The docks at Galveston, Texas, where Federal boats have landed.

VOICE-OVER OF JAMES FERGUSON: As I was saying—Granger had landed in Galveston . . .

GRANGER: The people of Texas are informed that in accordance with a Proclamation from the Executive of the United States, all slaves are free. This involves an absolute equality of rights and rights of property between former masters and slaves, and the connection heretofore existing between them becomes that between employer and free laborer. The freedmen are advised to remain at their present homes and work for wages.

KING: Remember this day, Ellis: It marks your freedom and my ruin. You're free. You're as free as me. You're free to starve and freeze and make your own way.

ELLIS: I know how to work. I won't starve.

KING: Where you going to work? I can't pay you. I don't have any money.

ELLIS: Then you're right, Mr. Hamilton. I'm as free as you.

ACT 3

Scene: June 19, 1995. At the Ferguson family reunion in Austin, Texas.

C.J. AND JOELLE: What happened to Ellis?

LANG: I'll tell it. There was Ellis and his mama Elizabeth and his brother Samuel and his sister Lilly. King Hamilton's father had sold Zeke and Zeke Jr. to two different plantations so nobody knew where they were. Samuel wanted to take off right away and try to find his daddy and his brother.

MICHELLE: But Elizabeth had a plan. King Hamilton needed help to get his corn and cotton in. She had children who needed a roof over their heads and food in their stomachs. She didn't ask King for money in return for work. She asked for land, free and clear, and she got it.

LANG: The family built a house and raised their own crops—enough to feed themselves and extra to sell. It got to where things got a little better, and King could pay them a little something for their work. He was a smarter man than his daddy was.

MICHELLE: Samuel did take off for Louisiana, but he never found Zeke or Zeke Jr. Lilly married Tyler James, and they bought a piece of land from King.

LANG: Ellis worked hard. At night, Tyler taught him to read. After Elizabeth died, the land was Ellis's. He stayed and bought more land from King. And when King died, he left Ellis a piece of property alongside the creek.

JOELLE (*to her grandparents*): The place where we swim when we visit you?

C.J.: King Hamilton gave that land to Ellis?

JAMES: Well, I guess King figured he owed it to Ellis.

What Happened?

Abraham Lincoln issued the Emancipation Proclamation on September 22, 1862. The Proclamation stated that all slaves in the states of the rebellion—the southern states—would be free as of January 1, 1863. Lincoln guaranteed that they would be given safe refuge in the North. Only enslaved African Americans in the southern states were affected. Many northern states had their own emancipation acts in place already. These acts, however, usually granted freedom only when the person reached 25 or 28 years of age.

While the Civil War raged, the southern states ignored the Emancipation Proclamation. Then the war ended on April 9, 1865. Federal troops led by General Gordon Granger landed in Galveston, Texas, on June 19, 1865. General Granger announced his intentions to uphold the Proclamation.

Many legends surround the history of Juneteenth. It is celebrated on June 19 in Texas, Louisiana, Oklahoma, and Arkansas, and sometimes in regions of Alabama and Florida.

Read All About It!

Berry, T. *The Day God Came*. Nashville, TN: Winston-Derek Publishers Inc., 1993.
Hamilton, Virginia. *Many Thousand Gone: African Americans From Slavery to Freedom*.
  New York: Knopf, 1993.
Stepto, Michelle, ed. *Our Song, Our Toil: the Story of American Slavery as Told by Slaves*.
  Brookfield, CT: Millbrook, 1994.

Read Some More!

Hopkinson, Deborah. *Sweet Clara and the Freedom Quilt*. New York: Knopf, 1994.
Taylor-Boyd, Susan. *Sojourner Truth*. Milwaukee, WI: Gareth Stevens Children's Books, 1990.

ACTIVITIES

Celebrate Freedom

Juneteenth is a celebration of freedom. Which other holidays do students associate with independence? Open a discussion by asking your class to share their favorite memories of independence celebrations. What do they do on holidays such as July 4, Juneteenth, and Cinco de Mayo? If they celebrated their own personal independence day, on which date would it fall? What was important about that particular day?

Politics and Proclamations

One of the reasons that Lincoln issued the Emancipation Proclamation was that he hoped it would bring a quick end to the Civil War. What other reasons do your students think Lincoln had for wanting to end slavery? Were they surprised by the politics behind the Proclamation?

June 19, 1865

Ellis Ferguson and King Hamilton both heard General Granger say that all slaves were free. Do you think they felt the same way about the announcement? Pretend to be each person. Write a diary entry for Ellis Ferguson and one for King Hamilton on the night of June 19, 1865. As an extension, you may wish to have students compare their diaries with the actual narratives of formerly enslaved people and former owners.

Ask Abe

It's September 22, 1862. Abraham Lincoln has just issued the Emancipation Proclamation. He's holding a press conference about the Proclamation. Your class has been transported back in time. Ask them to prepare questions to ask President Lincoln. They can then write newspaper or magazine stories about what Lincoln said.

North vs. South

The Emancipation Proclamation was aimed at the "rebellious" states of the South. What was life like in the North for African Americans? How was it different from life in the South? Ask half your class to concentrate on life in the North, and the other half to delve into life in the South. Students may focus on the time period during or after the Civil War. A specific person, such as Frederick Douglass may interest them, or perhaps they may choose to find out more about the Freedman's Bureau, the Underground Railroad, or the Exo-dusters who established communities in the Midwest. What conclusions do your students draw about the two regions?

"Great" Greats

Ellis Ferguson was 10 years old in 1865 when he heard about the Emancipation Proclamation. Where do students think one of their great-great-great-great-grandparents or other relatives was in 1865? Ask students to interview members of their family to trace their "great" greats. Have any stories been passed down, or any keepsakes? Students can construct family trees to show their relationships to their ancestors.

1912-1922
Immigration:
First Stop, Ellis Island!

By Michael Peros

Characters (in order of appearance):

NARRATORS 1-2
PAULINA SPIGOS: a Greek immigrant
IVAN ERDMAN: a Russian immigrant
NICOLAI ERDMAN: Ivan's son
INSPECTORS 1-4
COMMISSIONER CURRAN
STEFAN BRODSKY: a Polish-American
IDA BRODSKY: Stefan's wife
DOCTOR

ACT 1

Scene 1: 1912. In New York harbor, on the deck of a barge approaching Ellis Island.

NARRATOR 1: Millions of people left Europe during the late 1800's. They fled their homes because of hunger, religious persecution, harsh governments, or the lack of jobs in their countries. For these immigrants, America was a land of opportunity. Wages were higher, and land was cheaper. Many had heard that the streets were paved with gold! From 1892 to 1954, Ellis Island was the first stop in America for many immigrants.

NARRATOR 2: Meet three new immigrants—Paulina Spigos and Ivan and Nicolai Erdman. They've already been checked for illnesses such as yellow fever, smallpox, and typhus. The ships they were on stopped in the lower part of the bay. Then doctors boarded the ships and checked the passengers. Now they're being taken by barge to Ellis Island.

PAULINA: The Statute of Liberty . . . she's so beautiful. Can you see the lady?

IVAN: Thank you, yes.

NICOLAI (*to his father*): America! Everything will be fine now. Nothing bad will ever happen to us here.

Scene 2: Later that day. In the Great Hall on Ellis Island.

NARRATOR 1: As the immigrants arrived, doctors studied the way they walked up the stairs to the Great Hall. (This was known as the "six-second medical.") Then the doctors would do a more thorough exam. After that, inspectors asked the immigrants a series of questions. Chances were—if you were a man in good health, with no criminal record, and good prospects for employment—you'd be allowed to enter America within a few hours.

NARRATOR 2: The rules, however, were more strict for women who were traveling alone, like Paulina.

INSPECTOR 1: Your full name is Paulina Spigos?

PAULINA: Yes sir, Paulina Spigos. I'm from Greece.

INSPECTOR 1: The doctors tell me you're in good health. You're single?

PAULINA: I'm engaged to be married, to Spiros Paniotis of Chicago.

INSPECTOR 1: Uh-huh. And you know this Spiros Paniotis of Chicago?

PAULINA (*indignantly*): Of course I know him. I grew up with him. He came here two years ago with his parents. He says he is ready for me to join him. Here, it says so in his letter.

INSPECTOR 1: Do I look like I can read Greek? He's meeting you here?

PAULINA: No, Chicago is too far away. He works.

INSPECTOR 1: Uh-huh. Since Chicago is too far away, how are you getting there?

PAULINA: I have money for a train ticket.

INSPECTOR 1: Uh-huh. Okay, Miss Spigos, only a few more questions—how much is five and five?

PAULINA: Ten.

INSPECTOR 1: How do you wash stairs? From the top or from the bottom?

PAULINA: With all respect sir, I did not come to America to wash stairs.

INSPECTOR 1: I see. Your Spiros is rich, is he? You'll have someone washing your stairs for you? Is this what your Spiros has told you? You see, Miss Spigos, this is exactly why we don't like to let women in by themselves.

PAULINA: I've known Spiros all my life. I know exactly what my life here in America will be like. Do you want to know what my life was like in Greece? Do you care that I had no family there?

INSPECTOR 1: Just calm down, Miss Spigos. We just don't want you falling into the wrong hands. But you seem like a woman who can take care of herself. Just be careful. You can change your money here for American dollars. You can buy your train ticket here, too. Next!

PAULINA: Inspector? The stairs? From the top to the bottom.

Scene 3: Same day. An inspector's office on Ellis Island.

NARRATOR 1: About twenty percent of all immigrants were held for further questioning. About two percent were of these were sent back to their home countries. People could be denied entry into the United States for a number of reasons: if they had criminal records, medical problems, or if they might not be able to support themselves.

NARRATOR 2: Sometimes families traveled all the way to America, only to be separated.

INSPECTOR 3: Mr. Erdman, why have you come to the United States?

IVAN: We had to. It was very hard for us in Russia.

NICOLAI: Inspector, we are Jewish. Last year, our family was forced to move. My father found it harder to work.

INSPECTOR 3: What was your business, Mr. Erdman?

IVAN: I was a tailor.

INSPECTOR 3: How much did you earn?

IVAN: About ten to twelve rubles.

INSPECTOR 3: Hmmm . . . that's about three dollars a week. Nicolai, what kind of work did you do?

NICOLAI: I was a student—until the government said I couldn't go to school anymore.

INSPECTOR 3 (*to Ivan*): Do you have a job waiting for you?

IVAN: No, Inspector. We know that it is against the law to have a job waiting for us. But, well, my brother Leon is here. He is a tailor, also.

INSPECTOR 3: What does he earn?

IVAN: About twelve rubles—I mean twelve dollars a week.

INSPECTOR 3: Does he have a family?

IVAN: A wife, and four children. May I sit down? It's been a very long day.

INSPECTOR 3: The doc say your fingers are stiff and swollen. Probably arthritis.

IVAN: No, no, it's nothing.

INSPECTOR 3: Nicolai, what are your plans here in America?

NICOLAI: I am strong. There are many things I can do. My father will not have to work so hard here. I can take care of him.

INSPECTOR 3: You have twenty-three dollars between you. Your father is a tailor, but look at his hands—he can't work. And Nicolai, you have no job experience at all. Do you know how many young, strong men come into this country every day? I'm sorry.

(The inspector marks the letters "SI" on the shoulder of Ivan's coat.)

NICOLAI: "SI"? What is this?

INSPECTOR 3: Special inquiry. It means your father will be deported, sent back to Russia.

NICOLAI: But they will kill him! No! No, you cannot send him back!

IVAN: Nicolai, do not say anything.

NICOLAI: Papa, I am not like you. I cannot say yes to everything. *(to the inspector)* I will take care of him. I will earn enough money for both of us to live.

INSPECTOR 3 *(shrugging)*: Maybe you can convince the Board of Special Inquiry.

NICOLAI: What is that?

INSPECTOR 3: You explain your situation to three inspectors. They'll give you a translator if you want one. They'll decide whether your father can stay. Next!

(Bewildered, Ivan and Nicolai leave the Inspector's office.)

IVAN: Nicolai, we have been here a number of days. We have talked to so many people. I'm tired . . .

NICOLAI: Papa—

IVAN: Look at my hands. They're right. I can't work the way I did.

NICOLAI: You cannot go back to Russia!

IVAN: It's my home, Nicolai. Just as America will be your home.

NICOLAI: Please, Papa—

IVAN: No. My mind is made up. Now—go to the inspector. Tell him I want to return to Russia. I want to go home.

ACT 2

Scene 1: 1922. In the Great Hall of Ellis Island.

NARRATOR 1: Between 1901 and 1910, over seven million immigrants entered the United States through Ellis Island. The numbers dropped during World War I. But after the war ended in 1918, the numbers started rising. As a result, the First Quota Law was passed in 1921. This put a monthly limit on the number of immigrants who could enter the United States from any given country.

NARRATOR 2: Stefan Brodsky, a Polish-American man who immigrated to the United States two years earlier, is pacing in the Great Hall. He stops long enough to stare at the faces of the new arrivals entering the Great Hall. Commissioner Curran, who is in charge of Ellis Island, approaches Stefan.

CURRAN: Good afternoon. Are you waiting for someone?

STEFAN: Yes, my wife Ida, Ida Brodsky. She's coming in from Poland. Her ship's a day late.

CURRAN: How long have you been in America?

STEFAN: Oh, we've both been here for two years. Ida only went back to visit her parents. Her mother's sick. I only hope everything is all right.

CURRAN: No need to worry. I'm Commissioner Curran, and I can assure you that these little trips don't count against the Quota Law.

STEFAN: Thank you, Mr. Curran, but you don't understand—

CURRAN: You see, if your wife has already been admitted to the United States, and then she goes back to her homeland—well, when she returns to America, she'll probably be allowed in. Even if Poland's limit has already been reached.

(Ida Brodsky, carrying a bundle enters the Great Hall. She is accompanied by the ship's doctor and an inspector.)

STEFAN: I realize that, but you—

IDA: Stefan!

STEFAN: Ida!

CURRAN: What's that she's carrying?

STEFAN: I believe that's our baby. Excuse me, Commissioner. (*hurrying up to Ida*)

IDA: Stefan, look: He has your eyes.

DOCTOR: Mrs. Brodsky needs to stay here in the hospital tonight so I can check her out. The baby was born just last night.

IDA: Stefan, there's a problem—

STEFAN: What? What is it? Are you all right? The baby? What?

IDA: No, nothing like that.

INSPECTOR 4: The Polish quota was reached yesterday. To put it bluntly—the mother can stay, but the baby must leave.

IDA: My baby! They can't send my baby away!

STEFAN: Don't worry, Ida. No one will take our baby.

CURRAN: Are you sure the quota has been reached?

INSPECTOR 4: Yes, sir.

IDA: Stefan, if our baby can't come in, I will go back to Poland with him.

STEFAN: Mr. Curran. Please, help us.

CURRAN: Don't worry, Stefan, I'm sure we can work this out. (*to the Inspector*) Where was the baby born?

INSPECTOR 4: Aboard ship, sir. On the *Lapland*, of the British Star Line.

CURRAN: There you are! The baby wasn't born in Poland, but on a British ship. The deck of a British ship, no matter where in the world it is, is the same as British soil. Include the baby in the British quota.

INSPECTOR 4: Sir . . . the British quota was reached yesterday.

IDA: Our baby can't come in?

CURRAN: Wait, wait. You said the baby was born on board the *Lapland*? That ship's home port is Belgium. There! The baby is Belgian!

STEFAN: My baby is what?

INSPECTOR 4: Uh . . . sir? The Belgian quota ran out a week ago.

CURRAN: Inspector, whose side are you on?

INSPECTOR 4: Sorry, sir, just doing my job.

STEFAN: First my baby's Polish, then he's British, then he's Belgian! Now what is he?

CURRAN: Look here, I've got it. You see, with children, it's the way it is with wills. We follow the intention.

STEFAN AND IDA: What?

INSPECTOR 4: What?

CURRAN: Here's the thing. It's clear enough that Ida was hurrying back so that the baby would be born in America. And the baby had the same intention—he wanted to be born in America. But the ship was a day late, and that upset everything. So, under the law, this baby, by intention, was born in America. This baby is definitely an American.

IDA: Stefan. (*whispering to her husband*) What's your first name, Mr. Curran?

STEFAN: We'd like to name our baby after you.

What Happened?

Only a 27 1/2 acre piece of land in upper New York Bay, Ellis Island served as the first stop in the United States for millions of immigrants. From 1892 to 1954, Ellis Island was the main immigrant receiving station in the United States. During the peak years of immigration— between 1901 and 1910— approximately seven million people passed through Ellis Island.

Ellis Island was almost a city in itself; its facilities included a waiting room, dormitory, money exchange, hospital, dining rooms, post office, courtrooms, restaurants, a railroad ticket office, laundries, and charity and church offices. Most of the processing of immigrants took place in a large area which became widely known as the Great Hall. Immigrants would be asked a series of questions by immigration inspectors. The questions dealt with age, health, money, and prospects for employment. (An immigrant, however, often couldn't admit that she or he had the promise of a job. An 1885 law passed by Congress decreed that U.S. employers couldn't promise work to immigrants. It was feared that immigrants would accept lower wages than American workers.)

The immigrants were also given medical examinations; some were then referred to other inspectors who would test their mental capabilities. Most were allowed through within a few hours. About one-third settled in New York City, and the remaining two-thirds boarded trains for other destinations in America. But about twenty percent of the immigrants were detained for further questioning; approximately two percent were deported. People could be deported for a number of reasons: criminal records, health problems, or dim employment prospects. A Board of Special Inquiry, composed of three inspectors and an interpreter, would hear these cases. An immigrant could appeal this board's decision to immigration officials in Washington, D.C.

World War I aroused strong feelings against immigration in the United States. In 1921, a Quota Law was passed, which severely restricted the number of people who would be accepted into this country. As the number of immigrants steadily decreased, Ellis Island was utilized for other purposes, including a Coast Guard station. Finally, in 1954, it was boarded up and abandoned. In 1990, Ellis Island reopened is doors after a seven-year restoration project. The centerpiece of the restoration is the Ellis Island Immigration Museum. The museum is now one of New York's largest cultural institutions, attracting almost two million visitors per year.

📖 Read All About It!

Benton, Barbara. *Ellis Island: A Pictorial History*. New York: Facts on File, 1985.

Lawlor, Veronica. *I Was Dreaming to Come to America: Memories from the Ellis Island Oral History Project*. New York: Viking, 1995.

Levine, Ellen. *If Your Name Was Changed at Ellis Island*. New York: Scholastic Inc., 1993.

Siegel, Beatrice. *Sam Ellis's Island*. New York: Four Winds Press, 1985.

📖 Read Some More!

Freedman, Russell. *Immigrant Kids*. New York: Dutton Children Books, 1980.

Sachs, Marilyn. *Call Me Ruth*. New York: Doubleday, 1982.

Takai, Ronald. *Spacious Dreams: The First Wave of Asian Immigration*. New York: Chelsea House, 1994.

ACTIVITIES

Streets of Gold

In the late 19th and early 20th centuries, some immigrants believed that the streets of America were paved with gold. Now, late in the 20th century, how do your students think that people from other countries view America? Is it still the land of opportunity? Has America changed during this century? What do they think this country's immigration policy should be: accept all who want to immigrate or limit it?

You're the Inspector

Review the inspections which the characters in the play had to face with students. How would they rule on each one? Should Paulina have been held at Ellis Island until Spiros arrived to pick her up? What about the Erdmans—do students think that Nicolai could have supported his father? And just what nationality should have been given to the Brodsky baby?

Dear Paulina

That first sight of the Statue of Liberty must have been thrilling for many immigrants. It meant that their long journey was almost over. But imagine what it must have been like to set foot into the Great Hall on Ellis Island. Set up a situation where students pretend that they are interpreters at Ellis Island. They may choose one of the characters in the play to help. What would they do to make the character more comfortable? Ask the interpreters to write letters to the characters. They should share similar experiences (of going into new situations) with the characters. How did they handle their own experiences?

Breaking Up Is Hard to Do

Sometimes families would be separated when one or more members departed first for America. Ask students to write a short play in which members of a family must cope with such a separation.

Herring and Potatoes

It often took weeks of ocean travel to reach New York harbor. Those immigrants who passed through Ellis Island didn't travel first class. Conditions were difficult. Encourage students to find out more about what these journeys were like. Based on their research, have them write a series of journal entries by immigrants describing their journeys.

Leaving Trouble Behind

The high volume of immigration was often tied to difficult conditions in the immigrants' native countries. Have students research a country from which there have been a large number of immigrants. What prompted people to flee these countries? They may wish to concentrate on the countries mentioned in the play—Poland, Russia, and Greece—or on other countries, such as Ireland, Vietnam, Mexico, and Sweden. Also, encourage them to take a look at other ports of entry into the United States. Angel Island, Galveston, New Orleans, and Boston have received a number of immigrants.

1941
Pearl Harbor:
WORDS OF WAR

By Helen H. Moore

Characters (in order of appearance):

NARRATORS 1-2

LOUISE CAMPBELL: a teacher from the mainland

TOMMY NISHI: a 12-year-old boy

JOE CAMPBELL: Louise's 12-year-old son

LANE BEATON: a 12-year-old girl

TAKASHI NISHI: Tommy's father, manager of Beaton pineapple plantation

REVEREND SIMMS: the children's Sunday school teacher

HILDA BEATON: Lane's grandmother, owner of Beaton pineapple plantation

FUJIKO NISHI: Tommy's mother, bookkeeper at Beaton pineapple plantation

ED CAMPBELL: Joe's father, an American naval communications officer stationed in Hawaii

SAM DOBBINS: an American naval mechanic stationed in Hawaii

FRANKLIN ROOSEVELT: 32nd president of the United States

ACT 1

Scene 1: December 5, 1941. A sixth-grade classroom in Honolulu, Hawaii.

NARRATOR 1: In December of 1941, the Axis powers—Germany, Italy, and Japan—were at war with the Allied powers—England and France. Because of its experiences in World War I, the United States wanted to remain neutral and stay out of the war.

NARRATOR 2: The American base at Pearl Harbor, on the island of Oahu in Hawaii, was considered to be one of the best-defended bases that the United States had. The ships of the United States Pacific fleet were anchored there. The United States was neutral, but it hoped that the presence of the Pacific fleet at Pearl Harbor would make Japan think twice about its military plans.

LOUISE CAMPBELL: Who can tell us when Hawaii became a territory of the United States? (*ignoring her son Joe who is wildly waving his hand*) Tommy?

TOMMY: 1900.

LOUISE CAMPBELL: Very good. Now, who can tell us what being a territory of the United States means? (*continuing to ignore Joe*) Lane?

LANE BEATON: It means—

JOE CAMPBELL (*interrupting*): But what if the Japanese do attack Pearl Harbor?

LOUISE CAMPBELL: Joe Campbell! Is your name Lane? Did I call on you?

JOE CAMPBELL: No, ma'am . . . but—

LOUISE CAMPBELL: Since you want to know so much, Joe, I'd like you to write a report on Queen Liliuokalani and present it to the class on Monday.

JOE CAMPBELL: Aw, shucks, Mom!

LOUISE CAMPBELL: A five-page report, Joe Campbell. And I'll add a page every time I hear you using slang words in my classroom.

JOE CAMPBELL: Aw—aw—all right.

LOUISE CAMPBELL: Now, Lane, suppose you begin reading chapter twelve for us.

LANE BEATON: "Hawaii consists of eight main islands, and 124 smaller ones. They stretch across 1,500 miles of the Pacific Ocean. Oahu is the third largest island. Oahu means 'the Gathering Place' in Hawaiian. The majority of Hawaiians live on the island of Oahu. Hawaii's main crops include pineapple and—"

(*A loud siren suddenly wails, but Lane continues to read.*)

"sugar cane. The mild climate—"

LOUISE CAMPBELL: Thank you, Lane. All right, children, it's just another air-raid drill. Remember what we did last time? That's right—line up single file—no pushing.

JOE CAMPBELL: Nothing to worry about, right, Mom? Dad'll be okay, right?

LOUISE CAMPBELL: Right. Nothing to worry about at all. It's just a drill.

Scene 2: A few minutes later. In the air-raid shelter.

TAKASHI NISHI: Lucky we were in town to pick up the kids from school. There's not much shelter on the road to the plantation. A palm tree's not much protection against a bomb—

FUJIKO NISHI: Takashi!

REVEREND SIMMS: Mrs. Beaton, if I may speak bluntly, you're one of the few people who can afford to take your family to the mainland. The Japanese may attack any day. You'll be much safer in the United States.

MRS. BEATON: It's no good trying to frighten me, young man. I've lived here since 1900. I'm not going to be driven away now, by rumors of war.

REVEREND SIMMS: But what if the rumors turn out to be true, Mrs. Beaton?

MRS. BEATON: Nonsense! All the generals and the admirals and the-what-have-yous agree that if the Japanese were to attack—and I emphasize if—they would hit Borneo, or Thailand, or Manila. Pearl Harbor is too heavily defended.

LANE BEATON: This is my home, and I'm not leaving it. I don't care if the Germans and the Italians and the Japanese attack us.

LOUISE CAMPBELL: Well, the Campbells aren't going anywhere, either. Besides, if we were in any danger, my husband would know it. He'd have us packed up in a second.

JOE CAMPBELL: I'm not going anywhere! I'm staying right here with Dad.

FUJIKO NISHI: Besides, the Japanese ambassadors are in Washington, D.C., right now to talk peace with the United States. I think they'll agree to President Roosevelt's demands. They'll pull out of Indochina. They need American oil and gas.

TAKASHI NISHI: I don't know. It could be a trick. I was born in Japan. I grew up there. I can't tell you how many times I was told this: Japan has never lost a war it began with sneak attack. Never.

TOMMY NISHI: What if the Japanese do attack? What if I never get to see Granddad Nishi again? Dad, can't you get him to leave Kamakura and move here?

TAKASHI NISHI: I wish I could, Tommy. But Japan's his home. He doesn't want to leave it anymore than Lane wants to leave hers.

(Another siren sounds.)

LOUISE CAMPBELL: There's the "all-clear." Children, don't forget your books. Finish reading chapter 12 tonight.

TOMMY NISHI: Boy, she never forgets to give us homework.

LANE BEATON: Yeah. I bet if the Japanese did bomb us, we'd still have to turn in our math homework.

ACT 2

Scene 1: Sunday, December 7, 1941, 6:45 A.M. Aboard the USS Ward, a destroyer patrolling the waters outside Pearl Harbor.

ED CAMPBELL: The *Antares* says a sub's following them.

SAM DOBBINS: A sub! It can't be! That area's restricted.

ED CAMPBELL *(speaking into microphone)*: Antares, please confirm submarine sighting. *(listening as answer comes over his headphones)* Roger, Antares. *(to Sam Dobbins)* It's a sub all right, but it's not one of ours. Notify the captain.

SAM DOBBINS: He's already on deck. Looks like he's taking a look at the sub through the binoculars. Whoa! Hold on! We're firing! Too high! First one's too high—second one . . . got her!

(Both men hold on as the destroyer drops four depth charges.)

ED CAMPBELL *(into microphone)*: We have attacked, fired upon, and dropped depth charges upon submarine operating in defensive sea area. Over and out.

SAM DOBBINS: You don't suppose she could have been one of ours, do you?

ED CAMPBELL: I hope not.

SAM DOBBINS: If it wasn't, you know what that means, don't you?

ED CAMPBELL: It was a Japanese sub.

SAM DOBBINS: And what's a Japanese sub doing in these waters?

ED CAMPBELL: Spying on us, maybe.

SAM DOBBINS: Setting us up for an attack, is more like it. (*looking at the radar screen*) Whoa! Planes moving in fast! You'd better call Fort Shafter!

ED CAMPBELL (*into microphone*): Planes approaching, sir. Position is about 132 miles from us. Sir? Yes, sir.

SAM DOBBINS: Well, whose are they?

ED CAMPBELL: Ours.

SAM DOBBINS: Biggest flight I've ever seen show up on the screen. (*looking at the radar screen again*) Fort Shafter's sure that those planes are ours?

ED CAMPBELL: Yep. Duty officer says it's a flight of B-17s coming in from the mainland.

SAM DOBBINS: I hope he's right.

Scene 2: Same day, 7:50 A.M. Inside the Nishis' house.

TAKASHI NISHI: I saw that guy again when I was making my rounds this morning.

FUJIKO NISHI: Maybe he's just a tramp trying to sneak a few pineapples.

TAKASHI NISHI: A tramp wearing a suit and carrying a pair of binoculars? No. I think he's a spy. I better call the police.

FUJIKO NISHI: What would a spy be doing way out here? You'd think he'd be closer to the base. Why would the Japanese be interested in knowing how many pineapples Mrs. Beaton has?

TAKASHI NISHI (*shrugging*): You never know. He might not be the only one. He might be waiting for a signal or something.

(*Tommy, Lane, and Joe run through the front door.*)

TOMMY NISHI: Boy, you should see the planes coming in!

TAKASHI NISHI (*looking startled*): Ours? American planes?

JOE CAMPBELL: Sure. There are no sirens or anything.

LANE BEATON: Grandmother says she'll pick us up for church in an—what's that?

(*Through the drone of the planes flying overhead, they hear the sound of bombs exploding in the distance.*)

JOE CAMPBELL: But there weren't any sirens or anything.

(*A car stops outside. Mrs. Beaton rushes in.*)

MRS. BEATON: Hurry! We have to get to the air-raid shelter! It's the Japanese! They're bombing Pearl Harbor!

JOE CAMPBELL: Pearl Harbor! But my mom went to pick up my dad. They're both out there! I gotta go find them!

(*Takashi tries to grab Joe as the boy runs out the door. He goes out the door after Joe.*)

TAKASHI NISHI: Wait, Joe! Hold on! You can't go out there by yourself!

FUJIKO NISHI: Takashi! Come back!

TOMMY NISHI: Dad!

NARRATOR 1: Takashi and Joe hop into the Nishis' car and drive off toward Pearl Harbor. Thick, black clouds of smoke boil into the sky above the base. They can hear sirens, now—air-raid warnings, fire engines, and ambulances—and ships' horns calling crews to their battle stations. And Japanese bombers continue to fly in, dropping more bombs and striking the ground with gunfire.

NARRATOR 2: In that first round of bombing, Japan sent in 40 torpedo bombers, 50 dive bombers, 50 high-level bombers, and 50 fighter planes. Seven American battleships sitting in the harbor were seriously hit. American planes were knocked out of commission as they sat on their runways.

NARRATOR 1: At 9:00 A.M., the Japanese attacked again. A few surviving American planes managed to get into the air, but the battle was one-sided. In less than an hour, it was over. Half of the United States Pacific fleet was destroyed. Almost 200 planes belonging to the navy, marines, and army were lost. The number of Americans killed was 2,403, and 1,178 were wounded. The Japanese losses were light: 29 planes, 1 submarine, 5 mini-submarines, and 55 men.

ACT 3

Scene: Monday, December 8, 1941. Inside the Nishis' house.

NARRATOR 2: The Campbells, the Nishis, and the Beatons were lucky. Everyone survived, and no one was hurt in the attack. Sam Dobbins was seriously wounded in his right leg.

NARRATOR 1: America was stunned by what happened at Pearl Harbor. People spending quiet Sunday afternoons at home heard the news over the radio. They rushed into their yards and into the streets to share the news with their neighbors. Now Americans were ready to fight. The next day, people gathered around their radios, waiting to hear what President Roosevelt had to say. Congress had called a special session, and the president was going to speak.

FUJIKO NISHI: He's got to declare war against Japan. We're in it now whether we like it or not.

TAKASHI NISHI: It's time! Turn up the radio.

(The family huddles around the radio to hear what the President has to say.)

PRESIDENT ROOSEVELT'S VOICE (*over the radio*): Yesterday, December 7, 1941—a date which will live in infamy—the United States was suddenly and deliberately attacked by the naval and air forces of the empire of Japan. . .The attack yesterday on the Hawaiian Islands has caused severe damage to American naval and military forces. Very many American lives have been lost . . . I ask that Congress declare that since the unprovoked attack by Japan on Sunday, December 7, a state of war has existed between the United States and the Japanese empire.

TOMMY NISHI: But what about grandfather? He hasn't done anything wrong. It's not his fault that Pearl Harbor got bombed. He's not the enemy.

TAKASHI NISHI: No, he's not. Neither are we, but some people may not understand that. I was born in Japan. Some people may not trust me. Both you and your mother were born here in Hawaii. But they may not trust you, either.

FUJIKO NISHI: War is not so simple. It's not always easy to tell the good guys from the bad guys.

NARRATOR 2: Three days later, Germany and Italy declared war on the United States. World War II ended three years later, in 1945. And it was, truly, a world war: over 70 countries and 75 percent of the world's population were affected. About 20 million soldiers were killed and wounded. Tens of millions of civilians lost their lives or were hurt. What did the war cost? About one quadrillion dollars!

What Happened?

World War II started on September 1, 1939, when Germany invaded Poland. Two days later, on September 3, Britain and France declared war on Germany. A year later, Germany, Italy, and Japan signed a mutual assistance pact. Each of these countries—known as the Axis powers—promised to come to the aid of the others if they were attacked. The losses suffered in World War I made Americans leery of entering another global war, and the country maintained its neutrality.

In 1940, France fell to Hitler. Japan attacked resource-rich Indochina (today Vietnam, Laos, and Cambodia) and continued its conquest of Asia and the Pacific, which had begun in 1931 when it attacked Manchuria. The protracted fighting in China had depleted Japan's resources. Until the invasion of Indochina, Japan had gotten most of its goods—oil, gas, and metal—from the United States. But then President Roosevelt put a stop to trade with Japan. Trade would only begin again when Japan pulled out of Indochina. In response, Japan publicly opened up trade talks with the U.S. government, and privately planned attacks on American and British targets in the Pacific. Pearl Harbor was one of them. The raid on Pearl Harbor brought America into the war.

King Kalakaua granted the United States the right to use Pearl Harbor as a naval station in 1887. His sister Liliuokalani succeeded him to the throne. She was overthrown in 1893 by a group of American and European planters. These planters wanted Hawaii, now a republic, to be annexed by the United States. This connection would increase the profits from their sugar cane and pineapple plantations. Hawaii was annexed in 1898. The United States also wanted to strengthen its military position in the islands, and Hawaii became a U.S. territory on June 14, 1900.

📖 Read About it!

Salisbury, Graham. *Under the Blood-Red Sun*. New York: Delacorte Press, 1994.
Shapiro, William E. *Turning Points of World War II: Pearl Harbor*. New York: Franklin Watts, 1984.
Stein, R. Conrad. *World War II in the Pacific "Remember Pearl Harbor."* Hillside NJ: Enslow Publishers, 1994.

📖 Read Some More!

Bachrach, Susan D. *Tell Them We Remember: The Story of the Holocaust*. Boston: Little, Brown, 1994.
Marx, Trish. *Echoes of World War II*. Minneapolis, MN: Lerner Publishing Co., 1993.
Stanley, Jerry. *I Am an American: A True Story of Japanese Internment*. New York: Crown, 1994.
Watkins, Yoko Kawashima. *My Brother, My Sister and I*. New York: Bradbury Press, 1994.

ACTIVITIES

All's Fair in Love and War?

What did President Roosevelt mean when he called December 7, 1941, "a date which will live in infamy?" Ask students to look up the word infamy. Do they believe that Roosevelt was right? Then steer the discussion to what is fair and unfair in war. Is it possible for wars to have rules? If so, what kinds of rules should they have? How can those rules be enforced?

Evacuate or Stay?

Reverend Simms urges Mrs. Beaton to take her granddaughter Lane to safety in the United States. Tommy Nishi wishes that his grandfather Nishi would leave his home in Japan. How would your students react if they were in Lane's shoes? Would they evacuate to the mainland, or would they rather stay in Hawaii? What if evacuation meant being separated from their parents or relatives for a long period of time?

Headline News

Rumors were swirling around Hawaii in the days before the attack on Pearl Harbor. How do newspapers separate facts from rumor when they report the news? Or are rumors important to investigate, too? Ask students to write headlines summarizing each scene in the play. They may choose to create short, tabloid-style heads or longer, more descriptive ones. Then encourage each student to write a news story to accompany one headline. Remind them to differentiate between facts and rumors in their stories.

Where Were They?

Some students may have grandparents who participated in World War II, or your community may have a V.F.W. or American Legion organization whose members served in that war. Have your class compose letters asking veterans about their wartime experiences. You may also wish to expand this activity to include civilian reminiscences.

December 7, 1941—Around the World

The United States was neutral; but by December 1941, many countries were at war. Have students work on one of two projects: researching the key events of World War II to incorporate into a timeline that shows the course of the war, or collecting data to create a "war-and-peace map" of the world which shows which countries were involved in the war as of December 7, 1941.

Hawaiian Newscast

Have your students work in groups to create newscasts about Hawaii. Each group can focus on topics such as how Hawaii became a state, Hawaii's volcanoes, and tourism in Hawaii. Have each group present its newscasts to the rest of the class.

Civil Rights:
The Greensboro Sit-in

By Mary Pat Champeau

Characters (in order of appearance):

JOSEPH MCNEIL: Black college student

WHITE WAITRESS AT BUS STATION

NARRATORS 1-2

EZELL BLAIR, JR.: Black college student

FRANKLIN MCCAIN: Black college student

DAVID RICHMOND: Black college student

WHITE SHOPPERS 1-3 (nonspeaking roles)

WHITE WAITRESS AT F.W. WOOLWORTH

JERRY: Black dishwasher at F.W. Woolworth

WHITE POLICEMAN (nonspeaking role)

MR. HARVEY: White store manager

WHITE WOMEN 1-2

BLACK STUDENTS 1-3

WHITE REPORTER FROM *THE NEW YORK TIMES*

Scene 1: January 31, 1960. Luncheonette at bus station in Greensboro, North Carolina.

JOSEPH (*sitting down at counter*): I'd like a hamburger and a cup of coffee, please.

WAITRESS: Sorry. We don't serve Negroes.

NARRATOR 1: Unfortunately, Joseph McNeil is used to this kind of treatment. He leaves the counter without saying a word. That night, he is sitting with three friends in a dormitory room at North Carolina Agricultural and Technical College, discussing the incident. Joseph's friends share his anger and frustration. They decide they've talked about the injustice of discrimination long enough—it's time to do something!

Scene 2: The next day, February 1, 1960. Inside the F.W. Woolworth in Greensboro.

NARRATOR 2: Joseph and his three friends Ezell, Franklin, and David, dressed in coats and ties, stroll into the F.W. Woolworth, a popular shopping spot on Elm Street in Greensboro. They buy several dollars worth of personal items and school supplies. It's 4:30 P.M., and the store is crowded with shoppers.

EZELL: You know what? I feel like having a cup of coffee.

FRANKLIN: Funny you should say that. I was just thinking to myself how nice a hamburger would taste right about now.

DAVID: And I'm tired from all this shopping. The seats at the lunch counter look mighty inviting.

JOSEPH (*taking a deep breath*): Let's do it.

NARRATOR 2: The four friends walk over to the L-shaped lunch counter and sit down. A few shoppers are shocked to see black men at the "Whites Only" counter. They stop to watch what will happen next. The white waitress notices the students, but pretends to be busy. Several minutes pass.

JOSEPH (*finally speaking to waitress*): Excuse me, I'd like to get a cup of coffee, please.

WAITRESS (*not looking at him*): We don't serve coloreds here.

DAVID (*holding up a shopping bag*): I beg you pardon, but you just served me at a counter not three feet away.

WAITRESS: Negroes eat at the other end. (*She points to a stand-up counter where food is served to Woolworth's black clientele.*) Standing up.

EZELL: But we'd like to eat here, at this counter, sitting down.

NARRATOR 2: More shoppers start gathering outside the counter area. The atmosphere is tense. Everyone knows that black Southerners have paid dearly for this kind of "uppity" behavior in the past with jail time, beatings—and sometimes death.

JERRY (*approaching cautiously when the waitress turns her back*): Listen, boys, you all know the rules. Why make a fuss? Have your coffee over at the other counter where you belong and then get on home. You've already wasted ten minutes sitting here when you know you're not going to get served.

JOSEPH: Our people have wasted over 300 years sitting around waiting for something that nobody's going to give us. We can wait another hour or so.

NARRATOR 2: Suddenly, a white policeman enters the counter area and takes out his club. He begins patrolling the lunch counter, knocking his club against his hand in an attempt to scare the students.

JERRY (*speaking in a low voice*): If you were my sons, I'd drag you out of here while there was still something left to drag. All you're doing is asking for trouble, and you're likely to get yourselves killed in the meantime.

DAVID: If we don't do this, who will? I don't want my children growing up in a country where they're made to feel ashamed of their skin color. I want them to be proud, not ashamed or afraid.

EZELL: Besides, you don't see "Whites Only" on the dollars we spend in this town, do you? No, sir. Anyone at all will take our money, isn't that right, Mr. Harvey?

NARRATOR 2: Mr. Harvey, the store manager, has just been informed about the problem at the lunch counter and wants to resolve it quickly. His store depends on money spent by black shoppers. Although he doesn't want to offend the students, he has no intention of disobeying the Jim Crow laws. These laws forbid blacks and whites to eat in the same areas of a restaurant, drink from the same water fountains, use the same restrooms, or mix in public places.

MR. HARVEY: You boys look awfully smart to me. Y'all are in college, aren't you?

DAVID: Yes, we are.

MR. HARVEY: You're a credit to your race, and you're welcome at F.W. Woolworth anytime, anytime. You've made your point. You've gotten our attention. Now, I'm sure nobody here wants to see fine boys like yourselves get hurt in any way, any way, so how about you just go back to your campus and get on with your studies?

FRANKLIN: That's exactly what we'll do, Mr. Harvey.

MR. HARVEY: Good! I knew you'd listen to reason.

FRANKLIN: Just as soon as we get our coffee.

NARRATOR 2: Two elderly white women break through the crowd and come forward to pat the students on their backs.

WOMAN 1 (*whispering*): Don't back down!

WOMAN 2: You should have done this ten years ago!

NARRATOR 2: Other white shoppers begin shouting at the students, calling them names and threatening them. The policeman stands back as if he's inviting the angry hecklers to take matters into their own hands. The students remain calm and stay where they are until 5:30 P.M., when the store closes for the night. Outside the store, the four young men lock their fingers together and raise their hands to form a pyramid. In soft voices they recite the Lord's Prayer. They've challenged the system of segregation for one hour—and survived.

ACT 2

Scene 1: The following morning, February 2, 1960. F.W. Woolworth has just opened its doors for business.

WAITRESS: Oh no!

NARRATOR 1: More than twenty black college students—including Joseph, Ezell, Franklin, and David—come pouring into the store and then sit down at the lunch counter. They occupy all the seats.

STUDENT 1: Coffee, please.

STUDENT 2: I'll have the two-egg breakfast.

STUDENT 3: May I see a menu, ma'am?

WAITRESS (*flustered and angry*): Now, y'all listen to me. Mr. Harvey says we aren't going to provoke you, but we aren't going to serve you, either. So you can go on and sit there all day long for all I care.

NARRATOR 1: The students take out their books and begin doing their schoolwork at the counter. They do sit there all day long, much to the dismay of store employees and Mr. Harvey. White teenagers and some members of the Ku Klux Klan try to provoke the students to fight, but the students refuse. They end their sit-in that day with a prayer. That night, they begin getting phone calls from friends in other cities in the South. Reports about the "sit-in at Greensboro" have begun to appear in the newspapers.

Scene 2: Two days later, February 4, 1960. Lunch time at F.W. Woolworth counter.

NARRATOR 2: The counter is packed with more than fifty students, but nobody's been served. White students from a nearby women's college have joined the sit-in, now in its fourth day. Hundreds of black students have begun protesting at other stores in downtown Greensboro. Newspapers and television stations from all over the country have sent reporters to the community. In fact, Joseph McNeil is being interviewed by a reporter from *The New York Times*.

REPORTER: Tell me, are these sit-ins just another passing fad for you college kids?

JOSEPH: You tell me: Is the poor treatment of black citizens just another passing fad for the people of North Carolina?

REPORTER: It seems to me that this is about more than getting a cup of coffee at a lunch counter. What do you really want?

JOSEPH: I want what every man, woman, and child in America wants—to be treated with dignity and respect. I want a decent education, a good job, police protection when I need it, and the right to vote—maybe even hold public office. I want to be able to go to a hospital in an emergency and not be turned away because I'm black. I want to live and flourish in a free society, not be enslaved in my own country by prejudice, discrimination, and segregation. And, yeah, a cup of coffee at the lunch counter of my choice would be nice as well.

REPORTER: Are you surprised that these sit-ins have already spread to Charlotte, Raleigh, and Elizabeth City here in North Carolina—and as far away as Norfolk, Virginia, and Rock Hill, South Carolina?

JOSEPH: No, I'm not surprised at all. Have you ever heard of the Reverend Martin Luther King?

REPORTER: Yes, I have. He helped lead the bus boycott in Montgomery, Alabama.

JOSEPH: That's right, when Rosa Parks wouldn't give up her seat on the bus. Reverend King says: "The courageous acts of a few can spark a revolutionary response from others."

REPORTER: Is that what's coming? A revolution?

JOSEPH (*smiling as he looks out the front window at a crowd of protesters in front of a nearby clothing store*) No, sir. That's not what's coming. That's what's already here.

NARRATOR 2: By the end of the week, many stores in downtown Greensboro, including the F.W. Woolworth, closed their doors. Store owners and managers promised to rethink their segregation policies. Some of these stores couldn't afford to stay open without money coming in from black shoppers. Others closed because of the negative national publicity. Shopkeepers hoped the protest would eventually lose steam, but that didn't happen. Throughout the South, sit-ins quickly became a popular way of putting economic and social pressure on establishments which discriminated against black Americans. A few weeks after the sit-ins began, the F.W. Woolworth finally re-opened its doors. And at lunch time, blacks and whites sat together, and were served, at the same lunch counter.

What Happened?

Shortly after the end of the Civil War, the Constitution was amended to guarantee ex-slaves the full rights and freedoms of American citizenship under the law. After the Reconstruction period, however, when the last Federal troops were withdrawn from the South, southern legislatures began passing the so-called "Jim Crow" laws (named for a minstrel show character) to restore segregation of the races and deny black citizens the rights they'd recently been granted by Congress. During the Jim Crow era, interracial marriage was strictly forbidden. Schools, churches, neighborhoods, theaters, restaurants, hotels, libraries, public parks, and even telephone booths, were systematically segregated—not only in the South, but as far north as New Jersey and Ohio, and westward to California. By the early 1900's, it became clear that the post-Civil War policies had failed to bring about equality, and a group of young black men, led by writer/sociologist W.E.B. DuBois, banded together in protest, helping to establish in 1910 one of the first organizations of the civil rights movement, the National Association for the Advancement of Colored People (NAACP).

In spite of small gains made by activists during the following years, it was not until the mid-1950s and 1960s that most white Americans became aware of how serious and urgent the need for racial equality was. A nationwide upsurge of discontent among black citizens created a new consciousness in the mainstream. Sit-ins, protests, marches, and publications drew attention to the fact that life for most African Americans meant little or no education, no right to vote, menial jobs, inferior health care, poverty, and inadequate protection from hate groups such as the Ku Klux Klan.

From 1954 until 1965, the movement attacked racial discrimination with acts of nonviolent resistance. In addition to helping integrate public places, the sit-ins at Greensboro launched a youth movement which inspired high school and college students to become involved in the fight against racism. One of the most significant protests of the time was Martin Luther King's "March on Washington for Jobs and Freedom" in 1963, during which 150,000 people of all races, many of them students, converged on the capital to demand civil rights legislation.

As a result of the civil rights movement, segregation of public schools was declared unconstitutional in 1954; segregation of city bus lines became illegal in 1956; segregation of public accommodations was outlawed in 1964; a federal commission to ensure equal employment opportunities was established in 1964; and the right to vote for all Americans was put into law in 1965.

📖 Read All About It!

Duncan, Alice Faye. *The National Civil Rights Museum Celebrates Everyday People*. Mahwah, NJ: BridgeWater Books, 1995.

Kallen, Stuart A., and Rosemary Wallner. *The Civil Rights Movement: The History of Black People in America, 1930-1980*. Edina, MN: Abdo and Daughters, 1990.

Levine, Ellen. *Freedom's Children: Young Civil Rights Activists Tell Their Own Stories*. New York: G.P. Putnam, 1993.

Moore, Yvette. *Freedom Songs*. New York: Orchard Books, 1991.

📖 Read Some More!

Davis, Ossie. *Just Like Martin*. New York: Simon and Schuster, 1992.

Durrell, Anne, and Marilyn Sacks. *The Big Book for Peace: A Literary Collection*. New York: Dutton Children's Books, 1990.

Greenfield, Eloise, and Eric Marlowe. *Rosa Parks*. New York: Thomas Y. Crowell, 1973.

Taylor, Mildred D. *Mississippi Bridge*. New York: Dial, 1990.

ACTIVITIES

R-E-S-P-E-C-T

The civil rights movement helped people recognize that everyone should be treated equally and fairly. Spark a classroom discussion about respect with the following: Have you ever been treated unfairly? Talk about what happens when people don't respect each other. How do you earn someone's respect? How do you show respect toward others? When you meet someone who seems different from you, what can you do to try to understand that person?

Speak Your Peace

One of the most famous speeches delivered during the struggle for racial equality in America was Dr. Martin Luther King's "I Have a Dream" speech. Present the speech in class, either by playing a recording or video of the actual speech, or by reading it aloud. After students listen to the speech, ask them whether or not they believe Dr. King's dream has come true. You may also wish to have students distill their responses into one or more speeches.

Where Were You?

Since the sit-ins occurred in our more recent history, chances are that your students know people who were involved in the civil rights movement, or who remember the time well. What questions do they have about that period of the 1950s and 1960s? Involve them in drawing up a series of interview questions to ask family, friends, teachers, or any other willing participants. Depending upon the availability of equipment, students may tape or video record their interviews. Otherwise, students and interviewees might work together in writing down responses. Some people may have memorabilia they would like to share and discuss with the class.

F.W. Woolworth—An International Musuem

There are monuments all over the United States which commemorate important events and people in our country's history. In November 1993, efforts began to transform the F.W. Woolworth building in Greensboro, North Carolina, into an International Civil Rights Center and Museum. It is hoped that the project will be completed by 1998. Encourage students to create their own tributes to the sit-ins, either in the form of poetry, prose, song, or visual art. To find out more about the museum, you and your students may contact The Sit-In Movement Committee; 2025 D. Martin Luther King, Jr. Drive; Greensboro, NC 27406.

Jim Crow

Jim Crow was a minstrel character whose name came to symbolize segregation of the races. Send students on a trip back in time by having them find out what life was like during the "Jim Crow Era." Their results may take a number of forms: reports, plays, poems, or short stories. Encourage the use of illustrations, too.

Movers and Shakers

Many people played important roles in America's struggle for civil rights. Dr. Martin Luther King, Jr., Rosa Parks, Thurgood Marshall, Ida Bell Wells, Medgar Evers, and Fannie Lou Hamer are just a few. Let students choose one person on whom to focus. (They may also wish to find out what happened to Joseph McNeil, Ezell Blair, Jr., Franklin McCain, and David Richmond after the sit-ins.) When the reports have been completed and shared, students may wish to prepare a timeline highlighting the events presented. Also make a U.S. map available so that students may pinpoint the places mentioned in the reports.

Notes